PAJAMA INC.

PAJAMA INC.:

LEADING FROM HOME

CLARYL TRUZ

NEW DEGREE PRESS
COPYRIGHT © 2021 CLARYL TRUZ
All rights reserved.

PAJAMA INC.
Leading From Home

ISBN	978-1-63730-800-4	*Paperback*
	978-1-63730-859-2	*Kindle Ebook*
	978-1-63730-988-9	*Ebook*

*To myself, who aspired to create this book,
thank you.*

*To the one who is reading this:
you're meant for greatness.*

SOAR

CONTENTS

	INTRODUCTION	9
	BRIEF HISTORY AND REVAMP OF VIRTUAL WORK	13
PART I	**ATTRIBUTES OF A VIRTUAL LEADER**	**21**
CHAPTER 1	UNLOCKING THE MIND FOR SUCCESS	23
CHAPTER 2	THE LOVING BRAIN	47
CHAPTER 3	IMPLEMENTING THE SMART HEART	61
CHAPTER 4	RECIPROCITY OF TRUST	73
CHAPTER 5	POWER OF TRUST	81
CHAPTER 6	SETTING MARGINS	93
CHAPTER 7	GRAVITY OF FORTITUDE	109
CHAPTER 8	PROFESSIONAL IDEATION	123
PART II	**VIRTUAL WORLD ENHANCEMENT**	**139**
CHAPTER 9	TO SPEAK OR NOT TO SPEAK	141
CHAPTER 10	ENVIRONMENT CULTIVATION	159
CHAPTER 11	THE GUARDIAN	175
PART III	**SEEING BEYOND**	**197**
CHAPTER 12	FUTURE OF REMOTE WORK	199
	ACKNOWLEDGMENTS	211
	APPENDIX	215

INTRODUCTION

How do you keep your remote team motivated?

If you are one of the many leaders who were impacted by rapid change in 2020, you now are leading your team from home. Knowing human beings are social creatures and need to connect with others, how do remote leaders foster teamwork and connectivity in a spatially distant workplace?

Some of your team may prefer working in the office. Some are scared about the new challenges. Some may even feel isolated. How do you, as a leader, navigate all these changes and keep your team motivated to be successful at their work?

I experienced this drastic change myself, from being in an office with my coworkers to working remotely with little contact with the outside world. Before I got promoted, my team would have a daily fifteen-minute meeting, and that was it. We were expected to be handling insurance claims all day long, which is obviously a solitary task. Because of the lack of interaction between the team members and our supervisor, I barely knew my team members. Upper management seemed to not exist outside my direct supervisor.

It was lonely. It is basically working for the sake of getting some hours in, a very dry-cut experience. It did not feel like it was worthwhile. I did not connect with the company, so much so that I was ready to quit right before I got promoted.

Once I got the promotion, I was set to make changes for the team I am creating. With upper management, I had more time to connect with other coworkers since there were more meetings involved about running the business.

As a team leader, I was the one to decide how much interaction my team members would get. If I chose not to have the meeting, the team would be unable to connect. Imagine having to do a task individually and not knowing your team members. You would most likely not reach out for help. With that in mind, I set meetings for them to do work-related tasks as well as casual talks for them to get to know each other.

The open virtual office (online meetings with an open agenda) provided a watercooler effect and enabled the team to do informal discussions. The team shared what was going on in their lives. In some of the meetings the team talked about their kids, pets, or favorite places to go to. They had healthy debate and friendly competitions occasionally occurred—allowing the team to be human.

Not everything has to be work related.

I asked the team if they wanted to get rid of at least one of the meetings and they said no, stating they liked the meetings as they are. On some days, we even went past work hours, team members chatting with each other, and some open office meetings became like a Friday night out.

I joined an open circle with Joe Yazbeck, founder of Prestige Leadership Advisors and author of *No Fear Speaking*. In February 2021, one of his guests brought up a common issue that has been haunting most virtual leaders: how can we foster trust and build relationships? He said he was having a hard time building a relationship with his team members.

Well, I can tell you from my experience that in a virtual community, intentionally building a relationship is even more significant. It may require you to do one-on-ones. Picking the correct communication software for team members will allow you to better serve your team. This is one of the reasons why this book was created. This book was born because I wanted to solve the same issues plaguing virtual management.

The historic novel coronavirus pandemic not only questioned medical practices that can better serve the public, but also questioned work environment practices to keep the economy going; the people and the government turned to virtual work.

The tips and how-tos on this book will help managers engage with their team more effectively— learning from the examples of how other virtual leaders struggled and overcame their hardships. The book also touches on the psychology of virtual leadership and practical tips on how to be a successful virtual leader. Virtual leadership can be difficult, but you can make it easy for yourself and your team members by learning a few tricks here and there.

As globalization spreads, the more necessity there is for virtual work environments and virtual leaders. Virtual work is not a temporary solution but is part of the future to move the economy forward.

As someone who is new in leadership and working from home, I am able to provide you the insights that are foundational to leading a virtual team. My fresh eyes into the field does not bring the intricacies to the topic that years of experience would, but the people I ended up interviewing and those whom I learned from do have that experience. This book is a mixture of information sewn together from the point of view of an apprentice and a master.

After interviewing virtual leaders, from CEOs to entry-level management, about the struggles of a virtual environment, I've identified the key principles that a virtual leader needs to navigate uncertainties in a non-collocated workspace. This book is created to dive deep into virtual leadership and share my findings with you.

BRIEF HISTORY AND REVAMP OF VIRTUAL WORK

Leadership has evolved in many ways from the caveman days and the emperors of Rome to something accessible to the common man.

The recent evolution of leadership is its transition from in-person to virtual; both differ in the definition because of their geographic location. In-person is the conventional way of working, that is, at the office, leading team members face to face. In a virtual environment, coworkers are spatially distant and traditional principles of leadership may not translate fully.

According to Think with Google, in 2020 alone, Google searches related to "team-building" increased by 9 percent (Marinova, 2021).

So what happened?

What were the biggest movers and shakers that ignited this exploration on team building?

The switch from the conventional work environment to the virtual environment caused many leaders to question how they can build their teams.

The changes are accompanied by one curious question: What makes virtual leadership less successful than in-person leadership, or vice versa? How can we encourage an environment conducive to success?

HOW WE GOT HERE
(FROM TELEWORKING TO REMOTE WORKING)

Did you know that working from home is not a new concept?

Around the 17th and 18th centuries, home-based working took root through the putting-out system, a domestic manufacturing system, or the so-called independent contractors of that time. These subcontractors would receive raw materials and make them into a product in the comfort of their home, taking away the hassle of transportation and any undesirable conditions that go with commuting (Hering, 2021).

In the early 1970s, Jack Niles, the father of telecommuting, coined the term when he was working remotely on a NASA communication system (Hering, 2021). Around 1992, the Interagency Telecommuting Pilot Project was introduced to popularize the use of telecenters in government agencies;

in 2004, the government passed a bill that encouraged remote work arrangements. By 2009, the Telework Enhancement Act was passed, and a boom of telecommuting jobs arrived, with more than 100,000 federal workers working remotely (Allied, 2021).

The rapid onset of new technologies in the 20th century further solidified remote working (Powers, 2018). The advancement of technology has made remote working easy. Some of these advancements include communication technologies; one of my older coworkers mentioned she used to have one of those Motorola bag phones. She said she would have to carry this huge chunky phone with her to make a call. And now, we have our iPhones that are much lighter, smaller, and work more efficiently. Same with computers: from having a hunchback computer to having a laptop that you can carry on your way to your vacation destination. Technology has made it possible for you to work on a moving car as long as you have a hotspot and a laptop available. And so, in the 21st century, the world's workforce experienced an exponential increase of virtual work.

The explosion of remote work from 2005 to 2017 grew over 159 percent, according to an analysis conducted by Flexjobs and Global Workplace Analytics using US government data (from 2017, released in 2018). A whopping 7.9 percent growth occurred between 2016 to 2017, so interest in this workspace is gaining traction, and there was approximately 44 percent growth in virtual work over the last five years since the release of the study, a huge leap for growth in this sector overall (Boulder, 2019). As of 2020, over 4.7 million US workers are working remotely (Montana Department of

Labor and Industry, 2021). In the year 2020, the historic novel coronavirus pandemic not only questioned medical practices that can better serve the public, but also questioned work environment practices to keep the economy going; the people and the government turned to virtual work.

THE VIRTUAL TEAM

The 2020 the novel coronavirus pandemic caused a shift in lifestyle, as well. With statewide shutdowns, more and more jobs moved from the office to a work-from-home environment, thus introducing an influx of virtual employment.

Non-collocated workspaces or virtual jobs have placed stress on the team and team management. The spatial distance has made it impossible to gain physical contact, has limited facial expression interpretation, and has left most team members isolated. The situation creates a cycle of perpetual downpour of negative emotions that people will then bring to work.

Here are a few reasons why virtual teams struggle:
- Lack of serendipitous meetings with your coworkers in the hallway, meaning less social interactions.
- Lack of trust that employees are doing their job.
- Burnout when work and life boundaries fade away.
- Lack or mismanagement of operational system.

However, these issues can be remedied; doing so will allow you to create a productive team.

In contrast, here are some of the reasons that make a successful virtual team: Increased overall productivity. According to a survey conducted by ConnectSolutions around 77 percent of virtual workers say that they are more productive working from home (Sword, 2016). Second, flexibility—one of the great accommodators and the ever-so-enticing benefit to working virtually. The 2020 State of Remote Work report conducted by Buffer and AngelList shows that flexibility around schedule and where to work are the top benefits working remotely. Some other benefits include increased freedom, personal control, and loyalty to the company. A staggering 81 percent mentioned they would be more loyal to a company with more flexibility (Pelta, 2021).

The way you run your virtual team is one of the determinants of how loyal team members are. Virtual leadership *can* be easier and less stressful, but it requires a different approach. The difference lies in which attributes of leadership need to be strengthened and honed. Conventional and virtual teams differ in how they go about achieving these goals.

Teleworkers are presented with unique obstacles compared to that of a face-to-face (FTF) team. To be an exceptional team leader, you must have the technical skills as well as the soft skills. Virtual leaders then need to possess abilities to help the team navigate the virtual world. And in many ways, the fundamentals of leadership are still the same in a FTF environment and a non-collocated workspace.

As we navigated the new trenches that many of us virtual workers faced, 2020 was a year when virtual leadership was once again challenged. Challenged not because virtual work was new but because of the circumstances that compelled and introduced the world's workforce to the virtual work environment. This includes the forceful push to work remotely; working remote was not an option but a necessity.

The year 2020 changed people's lives, including my own. I found a chance to work as a business analyst, which turned to a promotion, allowing me to become a virtual leader, leading twenty remote team members. It was quite daunting to be in this position. Knowing that I did not have experience in leading a remote team, I searched for ways to help build my team.

Before 2020, I spent part of my days reading about self-improvement, which led me to leadership—its fundamentals and its principles. From videos to scientific articles, I searched and devoured information. The books I read allowed me to have an easier transition to virtual leadership, but I discovered that some face-to-face leadership tactics did not work that well, while others were more useful than before.

PART I

ATTRIBUTES OF A VIRTUAL LEADER

CHAPTER 1

UNLOCKING THE MIND FOR SUCCESS

What is the relationship between your mindset and your leadership behavior?

In 2019, Tae Kyung Kouzes and Barry Z. Posner decided to find out. The research sample was taken from a 360-degree online leadership survey from a global organization's database. The survey is composed of individuals in management positions providing information about their mindset orientation and leadership behaviors. The findings indicated "growth-minded managers consistently displayed more frequent use of leadership behaviors than did their fixed mindset counterparts." Managers with a growth mindset are more likely to "engage in various leadership behaviors, and improving leadership competencies" (Kouzes and Posner, 2019).

Imagine planting two of the same plant species—one plant is in a pot and the other plant in your large garden. The plant in the pot, at some point, will stop getting bigger as its growth gets stunted. However, the plant in the garden will get bigger and bigger. The small amount of soil can only contain a small amount of nutrients, thus providing fewer nutrients. Additionally, there may be packed roots, and the constriction prevents the root from spreading out, stunting growth.

Think of yourself as the plant. If you are the plant in the pot, the fixed space (fixed mindset) will hinder your ability to develop fully. You get less exposure to external stimuli (nutrients), and you only can move in the environment you know (pot). If you are the plant in the garden (growth mindset), you have more capacity to stretch out your rooting system, get more exposure (nutrients), and grow to become a healthier tree. We shall call this stretching ability neuroplasticity.

> *We are discovering that the brain has more plasticity over time than we ever imagined; that fundamental aspects of intelligence can be enhanced through learning; and that dedication and persistence in the face of obstacles are key ingredients in outstanding achievement.*
>
> CAROL DWECK, PSYCHOLOGIST, AUTHOR, AND PROFESSOR (DWECK, 2007)

What is neuroplasticity? Neuroplasticity is the brain's ability to adapt. It is the restructuring and reorganization that occurs as the brain responds to the environment. The more you exercise your brain, the better it is at making connections. Over time, brain exercises make you smarter.

According to neuropsychologist Celeste Campbell at Polytrauma Program at the Washington, DC Veterans Administration Medical Center, neuroplasticity "refers to the physiological changes in the brain that happen as the result of our interactions with our environment." The brain is constantly reorganizing itself as we go through life. According to Campbell, "The brain begins to develop in utero until the day we die, the connections among the cells in our brains reorganize in response to our changing needs. This dynamic process allows us to learn from and adapt to different experiences" (Campbell, 2018). The brain's complexity and ability to rewire itself is something that we should take advantage of.

Understanding neuroplasticity gives you the power to believe you can improve by knowing that nature and nurture play a role in your growth—so, *hack* your brain for success!

For each endeavor you do, if you want to succeed, you need a growth mindset, especially in an ever-shifting environment like the virtual environment. New tools are constantly created to make our lives easy. The tools we are using today may not be relevant tomorrow. You have to adapt, and it is up to us to train ourselves so we can use these tools. Looking at it long term, you will need a growth mindset to embrace new possibilities in your horizon and grasp the opportunity to develop yourself continually.

MY JOURNEY

My growth mindset journey began in my college years. I am an immigrant who came from the Philippines and lived in Canada for two years before settling in the United States.

A significant amount of my life was spent adjusting to new things. It was especially hard for me when I went to college during my second year living in the United States. Struggling to fit in and living alone for the first time forced my growth.

In general, I was just having a hard time. My search for different interests landed me on e-commerce. Mind you, I was not the best when it came to using computers. I barely used my phone at that point. During my journey of wanting to know how to do e-commerce, I found myself constantly failing.

At first, I used Shopify, where you can create your website and sell. I ended up selling less than fifty dollars on that account. It did get quite expensive, so I had to close my virtual shop. If you have created a website yourself, you know how hard it is to get people to visit the website. I was just not good at marketing; and doing Facebook ads was getting too pricey for my college pocket.

After that, I tried Teespring. Teespring is a website that prints out clothing with a design you create. I created a random design of a gray sweater with a cross symbol on the front and a quote in the back that said, "Work for God; the retirement benefits are great." When I was making this sweater, I was looking at YouTube, and watching how the person was creating their own design. Some required reverse engineering and ingenuity to create.

After testing my skills using Teespring, I was not interested in that type of business, so I left it. A few months after, I visited my account, and to my surprise, one item sold for forty dollars. Although I may have sold an item for forty dollars, my profit came out to be only four dollars. Teespring keeps the rest of the thirty-six dollars to fund the creation of the item. For fifteen minutes' worth of tinkering and zero dollars in investment, I must say, not too shabby at all.

I like business, so my entrepreneur journey in my college years did not stop there. This eventually led me to eBay. Experiencing my entrepreneurship journey through eBay helped me in college. It is not so much what I did, but more so who I became in the process—in this case, from someone who had a fixed mindset to someone who developed a growth mindset.

My journey with eBay started during spring break. I was sitting on the couch at home and thought of the fountain pen sitting on my bookshelf. So I got up and was about to throw it in the trash, when I paused. I had an idea! I went back to my seat and opened up my laptop, looked at the pen brand, searched it on Google, and what do you know, I found a similar one on eBay selling for twenty-nine dollars.

I quickly placed a piece of white paper on top of my laptop keyboard, placed the pen on top of the paper, and took a picture.

In a few minutes, I created an eBay account. In no more than an hour, I had my pen selling on eBay for twenty-four dollars. Three days later, before I was about to head to the airport to go back to college, the pen sold, and so began my eBay journey.

I would go at least two times per semester to a thrift store and buy some items to sell them for profit on eBay. I usually netted less than one hundred dollars per month, or if it was a good month like December, maybe around five hundred. It was a good side hustle; eBay had generated some spending money for me without putting too much investment into it.

I loved the learning process and figuring out how business worked. I had to tweak things and figure how to make it work better. Because of the failure and improvements, I was able to develop a growth mindset.

The cycle of failing, then trying again, failing, then trying again made me understand that yes, I did fail. However, I also learned. My brain then categorized failure as part of the success journey. The more experience I got, the better I became, which made me see success not as an end goal, but a constant process of revising myself to become a better version.

GROWTH MINDSET & E-COMMERCE
E-Commerce is part of the virtual world: to thrive, you need a growth mindset. Results do not come quickly, and constant revision is necessary. Because of this, I learned you need a growth mindset when leading a team—virtual or not. Since you are in a place of influence, it is part of your job to better yourself every day, because the better you are as a person, the better you will be as a leader. You have left the space of "I" and shifted to a "we" environment.

During my journey of self-development in college, I read a lot of leadership books. Most of the knowledge that people have are not innate but learned. Taking the time to learn something new allows one to expand their horizons. They never go out and blame themselves or wallow in self-pity for too long. Instead, when they fall, they take the time to process the information, then collect themselves and stand back up.

I have taken the same outlook when I fail. I acknowledge my shortcomings, analyze what went wrong, give myself a pep talk, learn from it, and move on. For me, failing is an opportunity to learn, and it does not define me.

Your failure is not what defines you. What defines you is how you react to adversity.

If you cultivate a growth mindset, you are constantly looking for the next step, taking all the lessons from your previous mistakes, cultivating a forever-student stance, and constantly pursuing learning. A growth mindset is a lifelong journey where you have to monitor your fixed mindset in certain areas and enhance it for growth.

GROWTH VS. FIXED MINDSET

Carol Dweck is an American psychologist known for her work on the mindset psychological trait. She earned her psychology PhD at Yale University. Dweck taught at Columbia University, Harvard University, University of Illinois, and Stanford University as a psychology professor. One of the pivotal points in her life is the glorification of the IQ back in her school days, which is part of her research motivations. She is famous for her book titled *Mindset: The New Psychology of Success*, where she talks and differentiates the characteristics of a growth mindset and a fixed mindset.

Carol Dweck found a school in Chicago where the passing grade was eighty-four, and if the scores did not reflect eighty-four and above, they would add "not yet" to the student's records. According to Carol Dweck, a "not yet" grade would give the individual a sense of understanding that they are in the process of learning the information, a notion of the learning curve (Stanford Alumni, 2014).

Dweck set out to do her research on children by giving them hard questions. Some accepted the challenge and reacted positively, whereas others felt grim about the situation.

> *Students who were not taught this growth mindset continued to show declining grades over this difficult school transition, but those who were taught this lesson showed a sharp rebound in their grades. We have shown this now, this kind of improvement, with thousands and thousands of kids, especially struggling students.*
>
> CAROL DWECK, PSYCHOLOGIST, AUTHOR, AND PROFESSOR (DWECK, 2014)

In her research, she found that children who believed their intelligence could be developed (a growth mindset) were far more successful than their counterparts, the children who thought that their intelligence was fixed (a fixed mindset). The growth mindset individuals had far greater brain activity when they encountered errors, which allowed them to integrate the information and analyze it to make corrections (Dweck, 2014).

Another study conducted by Aaron Hochanadel and Dora Finamore from Kaplan University found the growth mindset helps develop grit, allowing individuals to persist amid adversity and facilitate long-term goals in accordance with the conclusion made by Angela Duckworth, a psychology professor who studies grit and self-control (Hochanadel and Finamore, 2015). Dweck mentions that each individual is a mixture, a fixed mindset in one area, and a growth mindset in another area. Everyone must check what triggers them because a fixed mindset holds us back.

Everybody is a genius. If you judge a fish by its ability to climb a tree, it will live its whole life, believing that it is stupid.

ALBERT EINSTEIN, PHYSICIST

We can use the fish here as the symbolic embodiment of an individual. If fixed-mindset individuals think skills are innate and cannot be cultivated, they will not strive to learn new things. They view successful people as being born great, which is why they are thriving, instead of thinking that some successful people got to where they are because they continually strive to learn and improve their existing abilities.

If the individual has a growth mindset, they will think that they do not have those abilities "yet" and will strive to learn to be skilled at their craft. The growth mindset is the "not yet" mindset. It gives the individual the ability to move toward the future with endless opportunities.

You will identify a growth mindset culture in that teamwork and collaboration are prominent, the educated risk is welcomed, and learning persists. From Carol Dweck's business research, she found out that the differences between a growth mindset and a fixed mindset organization (Talks at google, 2015).

	Organizational Culture Based on Mindsets	
	Growth Mindset	**Fixed Mindset**
Employees	"Felt more empowered by the organization and more committed to it" (Talks at Google, 2015).	"Had one foot out the door waiting for the next highest bidder" (Talks at Google, 2015).
Environment	People "said their companies valued creativity and innovation. They really put their money where their mouth was. So if you took a reasonable risk and it didn't work out, [the] company [had your] back. [The] company values teamwork" (Talks at Google, 2015).	"The employees said the company talks innovation and creativity. But if things do not work out, then someone pays the price" (Talks at Google, 2015).
Management	"Their employees had tremendous potential to rise within the organization, become stars, and join management" (Talks at Google, 2015).	Organizations "are worshipping the talent, hiring the talent, and paying to keep the talent, but a few years later they are not saying there are a lot of people who have potential to rise in the organization. Either they've left or they do not have the potential anymore" (Talks at Google, 2015).

According to the study *Why fostering a growth mindset in organizations matter*, conducted by a culture-shaping firm Senn Delaney, a Heidrick & Struggles Company, "Those in growth mindset companies showed 65 percent stronger agreement that their companies support risk-taking and 49 percent stronger agreement that their organizations foster innovation" (Dweck, Murphy, Chatman and Kray, 2021). As a leader, you need to cultivate a learning environment where people are still held accountable for their actions. They are given a chance to improve in the future and not be unnecessarily blamed for each misstep made.

Cultivate an environment for growth. Use the power of *yet*. If individuals are not doing the tasks properly, allow them to learn and know that they have *yet* to learn what needs to be done.

When I look at my team's results and the results are not right, I give them the information they needed that will help them get the desired results. I tell the team not to worry if I provide them with some corrections on their work. It is not an attack on them as a person; it just means they did not find the necessary information and tools to produce the desired results. It is a constructive process; we will be learning together. After giving them more information and tools, I will not hold them fully accountable for their previous mistakes but will hold them responsible for future ones after I have clarified the expectations.

One must set the expectations but should not judge the individual's ability. Everyone has the potential to be much greater than they currently are. Those who follow through on improving and honing their abilities are the ones who get catapulted to success.

You can equip people with the tools they need to showcase their *genius*. Like a swordsman who practices his sword skills every day, the individual you lead will eventually reach excellence. Eventually, the student will become the master of their craft, and the teacher will once again become the student.

TECHNICAL SKILLS AND GROWTH MINDSET

Learning a new technical skill requires a growth mindset. The virtual space is full of different software, some more straightforward than others. When I was first introduced to bioinformatics, I had to use some software that I had no experience with, nor had I ever heard of it.

Bioinformatics uses software to understand biological data. It is a combination of computer science, biotechnology, molecular biology, statistics, and engineering. At first, I was extremely frustrated and confused. Luckily for me, before I had to do bioinformatics, I had gained experience selling online, done a lot of research, and eventually developed my tech skills, most especially training my troubleshooting muscle. My previous experiences made it easier to do my bioinformatics research using online tools.

If you are a virtual leader, you cannot even use the excuse of being too old or not interested in technology. As the leader, you have to know at least most, if not all, of the software you need to use with your team. You do not have to be the greatest with the technology or specialize in knowing every single detail, but you are still required to know them. For example, if you cannot correctly navigate Zoom or any video/chat conference software, it will be hard for you and your team to get connected.

You also need to know simple troubleshooting measures, such as fixing your internet or Wi-Fi during times when it is spotty. It requires you to have a competitive level of computer/technological literacy. My point is as a virtual worker, you will be challenged to enhance your technical skills, and with a growth mindset, it will make the process a little bit easier. This will undoubtedly enable you to do the learning necessary to achieve your desired skill set.

HOW TO FOSTER A GROWTH MINDSET: PLANTING THE TREE IN THE GARDEN

TAKE ACTION:
IF YOU ARE AFRAID OF WHAT YOU ARE DOING, JUST START!
Just do it.

NIKE

Take this quote literally. Part of what hinders people from growth is that they are afraid to do certain things. If you want to grow, you need to do something that you have not done before. It becomes this calling to go out of your comfort zone. Be comfortable with the uncomfortable.

All you need to do is begin. Analysis paralysis will take you nowhere. A characteristic of people with growth mindsets is they are not perfectionists. Now I am not saying they perform tasks without care. What I am saying is they are not fixated so much on getting the perfect result to the point that it hinders them from performing the task. This is because they are aware that, even if they were not to get the result that they prefer, they have gained the experience and knowledge by doing. A win-win situation.

With my journey of entrepreneurship starting in college, my growth mindset came along with this experience. I started to figure out ways to make money online which, brought me to eBay. This was quite a feat for me to do back then. In the beginning stages I had a fixed mindset telling myself often that I could not do this because I was not talented or smart enough. What pushed me through pursuing what I needed to do were the motivational videos I used to watch. They often mentioned that a part of success is failure and to experience both is to take action. If you have not failed, you have never challenged yourself enough to grow.

Thomas Edison took many tries until he was able to get the light bulb working.

I have not failed. I've just found ten thousand ways that won't work.
THOMAS EDISON, AMERICAN INVENTOR AND BUSINESSMAN

As I tried different ways to sell products online, I found myself in a situation in which I came to accept that my talent and abilities can be improved through persistent effort. From then on, I was never afraid to do new things because I knew if I gave myself more time to learn, I would eventually know how to perform the tasks to be successful in my endeavors.

LOVE AND EMBRACE FEEDBACK

The human brain reacts differently to feedback when in a state of growth mindset because it encourages a person's openness to and integration of feedback and increases their intrinsic motivation to learn and perform.
DERLER, SANDERS, AND STEEL, 2019

According to the research *Transforming Performance Management with a Growth Mindset Approach*, "Modern approaches to performance management identify feedback as a critical element" (Derler, Sanders, and Steel, 2019). Regular check-ins, such as one-on-ones with your team member, will allow you to provide any course corrective feedback they can leverage for further improvement.

Bristol Myers Squibb, an American pharmaceutical company founded in 1887, piloted a growth mindset culture to 1,300 employees. The pilot became such a success that it had expanded to twenty-four hundred of its employees. Part of the initiative was to improve its feedback process. In the survey, 88 percent of employees and 97 percent of managers mentioned one-on-one conversation improved performance. Moreover, 93 percent of employees said colleague feedback helped improve performance (Derler, Sanders, and Steel, 2019).

According to a study done by the NeuroLeadership Institute, "Constructive feedback can be a catalyst for growth, and 60 percent of employees want regular feedback from their bosses" (Derler, Sanders, and Steel, 2019). One thing you can do as well is to get people to own the learning process. Have the team members reach out to you for feedback instead of proactively pushing it to them.

Based on experience, here is my take on feedback: I absolutely love constructive feedback. These tend to be the things that you happen to have no idea that you are doing wrong and someone happens to enlighten you about it. It creates room for improvement that you can work and tweak to improve. It's hard to do the right thing if you do not even know you were doing it wrong to begin with. Even if I get feedback, it is not always easy to change my ways of going about doing things.

So how should you provide constructive feedback? Part of what I found makes feedback helpful is when someone tells me what the issue is that required the feedback and gives me suggestions about what methods to do to improve the situation. Although you get the information about what you did wrong, if one has always thought that was the correct thing to do, it is hard to change and shift one's mind. So explaining it to the individual and providing other ways to go about doing the work helps.

Constructive feedback is like a seed. Once you notice the existence of the seed, you can nurture it and make it grow. If you were told you have a bad seed on your hand, then you can simply throw it away. You can call this feedback "food for thought"; engorge on it and take advantage of the information that you have been given. Growth-minded individuals respond better when feedback is given, and they pay more attention to mistakes while fixed minded individuals avoid constructive feedback altogether (Derler, Sanders, and Steel, 2019).

LEARNING ALSO INVOLVES SOME UNLEARNING

You need to tear down your previous beliefs and rebuild back up. In the movie *2012* there was a scene in which a monk teaching his student was pouring tea in a cup but never stopped. The student said, "It is full, great Rinpoche," the monk then replied to his student that "like this cup…you are full of opinions and speculations. To see the light of wisdom, you first must empty your cup" (Dmitri, 2017).

Like a tower made of Legos, one has to deconstruct to reconstruct. Reconstruct yourself, tear down the old beliefs that you thought were correct but are wrong or no longer relevant.

This requires openness on your part. Accepting that what you held to be the truth may not necessarily be relevant enough to be applied to the current situation.

A growth mindset approach enables evaluators to consider new data points, and to change their perspective and initial judgment about an employee's performance over time.

DERLER, SANDERS, AND STEEL, 2019

Leaders with a growth mindset are better evaluators. Unconscious bias often leaves inaccurate evaluations. According to the NeuroLeadership Institute study, "77 percent of HR executives believe that performance reviews don't correctly reflect employees' contributions," which may potentially leave some prospective star quality people off the table (Derler, Sanders, and Steel, 2019).

Growth-minded leaders accept contradicting performance information, are open to new data, great observers of decline or incline of work performance, place fewer labels based on initial impression, and provide assessment based on current conditions. These leaders take a more developmental approach using the current data they gathered.

Google LLC, a technology company, founded in 1998, introduced Project Oxygen in 2009. From its internal research, it found growth mindset tops the list of desirable manager capabilities in the framework. Managers "learn to challenge biases and existing assumptions, be more humble in their convictions, and try to reach informed decisions." Data speaks and will challenge some biases. Focusing more on a data-driven approach for their performance management strategy (Derler, Sanders, and Steel, 2019).

Google's management team focuses on employee potential and expands on the importance of room for growth. Google's success in being the "best company to work for…may well be a result of the company's performance management system" (Derler, Sanders, and Steel, 2019). Google's management practices are worth practicing; if growth mindset is on the top of the list, then it is definitely worth noting.

Here is a scenario of what an unconscious bias would look like:

I was talking to one of the supervisors that I work with, and she shared with me about an encounter she had with a team member:

Agent the previous day: May I request time off on Friday?

Supervisor: No, you have been asking for a request too often.

Agent: I might be absent tomorrow (Friday) because I had my COVID-19 vaccine today.

Supervisor (thoughts): The supervisor, already knowing the agent wanted to be off on Friday previously and considering they said they might be off, did not like the situation and had a talk with the agent on attendance. When the supervisor got her COVID-19 vaccine, she could still go to work the next day based on her experience. The supervisor felt that the agent was lying to her.

I personally was not thinking much about the issue until an agent of mine did the same thing.

Agent: I may be out the day after tomorrow since I have my COVID-19 vaccine tomorrow.

Me: Ok, keep me posted.

For me, I know this agent in my team rarely takes a day off and will only do so when necessary. I also did not have the experience of getting the COVID-19 vaccine yet, and I have heard mixed information about people being unable to work the next day and some being able to work, so there is a possibility of her being unable to come to work.

Two of the same situations resulted differently, mainly because of the unconscious bias we already had. The other supervisor has data to prove the agent is not performing well attendance-wise, which is why she took the necessary actions to lead her team the way she did.

Sometimes to understand something fully you have to challenge assumptions, unconscious bias, or beliefs. Part of the learning process is to unlearn some of your old beliefs. By using current information and data-oriented information, you will most likely be able to generate a robust evaluation.

PROCESS AND RESULT FULFILLMENT
Enjoy the journey, not only the destination. Part of what makes a process of doing something new less daunting and overwhelming is understanding that even if you were to not get your end goal, throughout the process you were

honing your skills and abilities and stretching your learning capabilities.

This method of thought will convert the notion: *it is a waste of time* into *time well spent*. Enjoy the means to the end, not just the end alone. People get so fixated on the result that when they fall short in fulfilling what they wanted to get, it makes the fall immensely hard.

Recognize effort and progress. Whilst rewarding positive performance outcomes is important, always acknowledge the effort that led to success, as well as the progress that has been made on the way.

DERLER, SANDERS, AND STEEL, 2019

PRAISE THE EFFORT

Praise the effort it took to get the result, not necessarily just the result itself.

By praising the process, you are positively reinforcing the action. You do not want the focus to be on the result, you want the focus to be on the positive behavior that helped produce the result. This reminder is helpful, especially when teaching others about the growth mindset.

If you want to foster the growth mindset in someone, have them act in a manner that produces growth. It may be as simple as supporting measured risk-taking behavior. People who tend to narrowly focus on the result are fixed-minded people. They only tend to think about the result and lose sight of the progress they are actually making. By praising the effort, it produces a lifelong influence for the person. The more they practice the behaviors that they are doing, the better they become.

> *Process praise keeps students focused, not on something called ability that they may or may not have and that magically creates success or failure, but on processes they can all engage in to learn.*
>
> CAROL DWECK, PSYCHOLOGIST, AUTHOR, AND PROFESSOR (DWECK, 2007)

I tell my team members "love the creativity" or "great observation" or "thank you for trying that out"—this improves motivation and makes the individual more willing to perform better. By saying "love the creativity," you are encouraging the person to become more creative. In comparison to you just saying "I love your painting," you are giving the person a momentary feeling of pride and achievement but will also make the person more cautious in creating less valued work.

Carol Dweck said students who have a growth mindset "understand that their talents and abilities can be developed through effort, good teaching, and persistence. They don't necessarily think everyone's the same or anyone can be Einstein, but they believe everyone can get smarter if they work at it" (How a Growth Mindset and Neuroplasticity Boosts Learning, 2020). A growth mindset can be beneficial to the team.

I emphasize growth as one of the foundations that a leader needs, since, more often than not, your potential is another limitation to your team members. Further along in the book, I will mention that I have the tendency to keep to myself. Well, guess what? As soon as I started talking to people, more opportunities came. I was able to have more visual on other projects that I could offer to my team members, which allowed them to have the ability to be seen. Sometimes our own limitations can and will limit the team.

A team culture with a growth mindset will "show higher levels of trust, empowerment, and collaboration" (Derler, Sanders, and Steel, 2019). Trust and empowerment are both key ingredients in maintaining a relationship with your virtual team. A growth mindset will help the team with engagement. Being physically distant already creates a barrier in getting the team engaged with each other. If a growth mindset culture fosters collaboration, then grab as much help as you can get.

As you lead your virtual team, aside from the solitary issue, you will find out autonomy is an essential aspect of the virtual work environment. Trust and empowerment will allow you to provide autonomy to your team members. A growth mindset helps with team collaboration and overall performance.

According to a study of several *Fortune* 1000 companies conducted by culture-shaping firm Senn Delaney, a Heidrick & Struggles company, an organization that practices a growth-mindset culture increases trust, engagement, innovation, and ethics. Employees have greater confidence in their companies and an increased sense of ownership in their work. Employees are "more committed to their company and more willing to go the extra mile for it, 34 percent likelier to feel a sense of ownership and commitment to the future of the company." Employees mention that growth mindset companies are supportive of measured risk-taking behaviors, such as innovation (Dweck, Murphy, Chatman and Kray, 2021).

On the subject of leadership and influence, I also find that, over time, people seem to have a negative connotation around the subject influence; it feels like you are manipulating others. I say the only thing that separates you from the good or bad is your intentions. Great intentions require an individual to foster themselves to be better, and that requires growth. It requires a person to figure out and filter through what is good and bad for humanity as a whole.

If you are in a position to influence others, self-growth becomes a responsibility. It is no longer an indulgence, but a responsibility, because if you are not growing yourself, how can you help uplift others to show their potential? You are in a position of service, and the better person you are, the better you can serve those around you.

A growth mindset will allow you to reflect the same mindset to your organization. A growth mindset will not only improve the individual but also the company. Pushing for a growth mindset culture at work allows you to offer a better feedback system to your team members or peers that will help improve performance. Growth mindsets foster trust, collaboration, and empowerment, which are key factors that will help keep team members engage in a virtual work environment context.

A growth mindset allows you to breakdown biases, thus providing better evaluations. Knowing you are constantly growing and that others are constantly bettering themselves places you in a position to consider that everyone has the potential and for you to provide coaching. A growth mindset expands one's horizon. The vast openness is a room for development.

Like the plant in the garden, a growth mindset allows one to flourish and bloom, constantly magnifying one's potential.

KNOWLEDGE NUGGETS:
- **Technical Skills and Growth Mindset.** The rapid growth of technology will require one to continue learning. Develop your troubleshooting skills and keep on learning.
- **TAKE ACTION: If you are afraid of what you are doing, JUST START!** Just do it.
- **Love and Embrace Feedback.** Learn to accept your shortcomings and polish your skills to improve.
- **Learning Also Involves Some Unlearning.** Let go of some of the biases and learn to see things in a different perspective.
- **Process and Result Fulfillment.** Enjoy both the journey and the destination.
- **Praise the Effort.** Praise and appreciate the process that people took to get to where they are.

CHAPTER 2

THE LOVING BRAIN

What happens when the heart and the brain merge as one?

We get emotionally intelligent individuals. Emotionally intelligent leaders benefit the team by motivating them and serving as a transformational influence. According to the research done by Prati et. Al about *Emotional Intelligence, Leadership Effectiveness, and Team Outcomes,* emotionally intelligent leaders "challenge the members of the team to work toward increasing team effectiveness and performance, facilitate team member interaction dynamics, build interpersonal trust, and inspire team members to implement the articulated vision" (Prati, Douglas, Ferris, Ammeter, and Buckley, 2003). Creating a space for improvement and interaction benefits everyone involved.

Emotional intelligence is necessary in understanding our relationship with others and ourselves.

Emotional intelligence is not about IQ but about how well we handle ourselves and our relationships, how well we work in a team, and our ability to lead other people. It is our ability to recognize our feelings and those of others, to motivate ourselves, and to manage our emotions.

DANIEL GOLEMAN PSYCHOLOGIST, AUTHOR, AND SCIENCE JOURNALIST (GAUTAM & KHURANA, 2019)

Leadership starts with yourself. You cannot go on a leadership journey, or any journey for that matter, without knowing yourself first. By knowing and understanding oneself you can truly strive to thrive in being a great leader. A lot of great leaders are highly self-aware. They are aware of their own emotion and are able to manage them to form even stronger relationships with others.

Leadership revolves around relationships, with yourself and with others. Emotional intelligence is an individual's capacity to understand their internal and external environments.

According to Gardner and Qualter, emotional intelligence revolves around the intrapersonal and interpersonal (Srivastava, 2013). Interpersonal intelligence is the capability of an individual to be self-aware and to have self-management capabilities. Interpersonal intelligence is the ability to understand others. Emotional intelligence (EI) is a useful marker in identifying a successful leader. A study conducted at the Johnson & Johnson consumer and Personal Care Group revealed that the high-performing managers have high EI levels in the domains of: self-awareness, self-management, social skills, and organizational savvy (Cavallo and Brienza, 2006).

SELF-AWARENESS

Yesterday I was clever, so I wanted to change the world. Today I am wise, so I am changing myself.

RUMI, PERSIAN MUSLIM POET, JURIST, ISLAMIC SCHOLAR, AND THEOLOGIAN

Why talk about self-awareness? Well, self-awareness is where EI begins.

Self-awareness enables one to identify the emotion and label it appropriately, reflecting on the next course of action.

Self-aware individuals also perform better at work, are confident, creative, are better communicators, are more likely to be promoted, and are more effective leaders with more profitable companies. They are also more fulfilled and have healthier relationships. In fact, 95 percent of people think they are self-aware, but only 10 to 15 percent of people are actually self-aware (TEDx Talks, 2017). In addition, the assessment done by TalentSmart, a global consulting firm specializing in emotional intelligence (EQ) training, discovered only a little over 36 percent of people were able to identify their emotions accurately as they occur (Bradberry, 2021).

When I was trying to set up my very first team, I made a mistake. When I started to observe my team was constantly asking questions and waiting for my answer rather than getting the answer themselves, I became aware of the mistake I made and was able to solve it. My mistake was building an environment where my team became dependent on me, because I gave them the answer immediately. This resulted in me having to micromanage the project we were assigned to perform.

The environment I created was one where people can constantly ask questions. The problem was I did not take into account some of the team members not liking to make decisions. Therefore, in every twist and turn, they asked for my opinion. This did not elicit a productive and effective team effort. Not only that, if I want them to be leaders as well, I have to encourage them to become independent thinkers and creators. I want the group to be a leadership mastermind, for the team to learn and practice their leadership skills then apply those learnings to their future endeavors. So, I had to change the working environment. I then started to train individuals on my team on how to do a search for information that can help them better decide. I had to do this myself first and had them follow me. I did not tell them how things should be done; I showed them how it should be done, and they eventually picked up on the habit.

Luckily, I was able to identify what I was feeling; unfortunately, I was feeling disappointed. It made me feel horrible, knowing that my team was being so dependent. Since this was my first time leading a team, I was reflecting on what I was doing and what was happening. I eventually figured out that the way I built my team might thrive in the short term, but it would crumble in the long run. I ultimately converted my team to become an independent one. Had I not reflected on my actions and the effects I have on my surroundings, things would have turned sour. My self-awareness allowed me to catch the error and remedy it.

Leadership involves having people become the best versions of themselves. So when I found out about this, I had to slowly convert my team from being dependent to being independent.

I created an environment that allows them to practice their troubleshooting skills. Instead of giving them the answers directly, I would give them all the information necessary for them to make a successful decision. It turned out well.

Once they are more accountable to their decision, they needed less of me. They were able to flourish as individuals within the organization.

SELF-MANAGEMENT
Self-management or emotional self-regulation allows one to adjust their emotions. If you lack self-control, you are at the mercy of your impulse. A person who manages his emotions becomes the master of it, and one who cannot becomes a slave to it.

Holding yourself against evocative stimuli allows you ample time to think before responding to the situation. This is useful, especially when dealing with other people. Self-regulation needs the individual to "understand the social expectation, and exercise discretion in the manifestation of emotions." Self-regulation allows an individual to be a functioning member even when turnover, conflicts, or other detrimental team situations occur, acting in a constructive and controlled manner (Prati, Douglas, Ferris, Ammeter, and Buckley, 2003).

I had a professor in college to whom I asked question after question after question. She expressed anger in a split second, then surprisingly enough, raised her pointer finger to point to the ceiling, inhaled, then exhaled, and had her emotions in check the next second.

I was extremely impressed. I have never seen an individual who had their emotions reined in as effectively as she did. Had she not been able to keep her emotions in check, our conversation would have turned into a debate. Aside from managing her emotions, she was also able to provide me the answers I needed. She managed to rein in her emotions, establish a solution for the question, and salvage the relationship. Self-management allows you to adapt to the changing situation and come out intact. It is a skill that can be learned and useful for the individual and others.

SOCIAL AWARENESS
Social awareness is being able to understand what is going on around you. Empathy is part of social awareness. Empathizing with other people allows you to see things through their lens and fully understand their situation. In a team, you need to foster an environment of collaboration. Without empathy, you will have a hard time getting people to collaborate. You can properly serve and lead if you know how to interact with the individual.

To lead, you need to be able to influence those in your care; otherwise, you will just be bossing them around. Authentic leadership comes about when the individuals follow you because you are one of them—a part of the team—and not because of your position. Influencing goes both ways, and empathy is a necessity to understand each other.

Emotional intelligence allows an individual to understand another. It allows you, the leader, to understand and see the potential each team member brings. The *Study on Emotional*

Intelligence At Work Place concluded that emotional intelligence brings "better adaptability, empathy towards employee, leadership qualities, participative management, decision making, and understanding amongst colleagues" (Kannaiah and Shanthi, 2015).

When I was working as a salesperson, I had a customer come up to me and asked, "Which shoe do you like better, the blue one or the black one?" I answered, "The black one." I also mentioned that I had one other customer who had an issue with the fitting near the ankles for this model and for her to try the shoe to see if it fits her. It worked out for her, and she bought the shoe.

She was so impressed with my honesty, she asked me to help her make further purchases in the store, which amounted to around $1,000 worth of merchandise. Emotional intelligence showcases empathy. At that time, I was thinking, *Well, if I were buying the shoe, I would want to make sure that it does not have any problems.* Now that's what I call placing myself in someone else's shoes—no pun intended, I just couldn't resist. I was also aware one customer had a fitting issue and wondered, *Why not have her check it first?*

Why did I do this? For one, I wanted a satisfied customer. Two, if a person is not satisfied with their purchase, they will be bound to return the merchandise. I often see some coworkers lavishly praising the product to get a sale, only to have the merchandise returned a few days later. The funny thing is, in retail, it is not the product you should be trying to sell; it is how the product can provide value to the customer, which is why you need to understand who your customer is and what their needs are at the time.

Empathizing with my customer and viewing things through her lens enabled me to provide a more authentic review of the product, and in return, I got a satisfied customer. Empathy helps you build a connection with others. Emotional intelligence gives one the ability to navigate through the social environment.

PSYCHOLOGICAL NEEDS

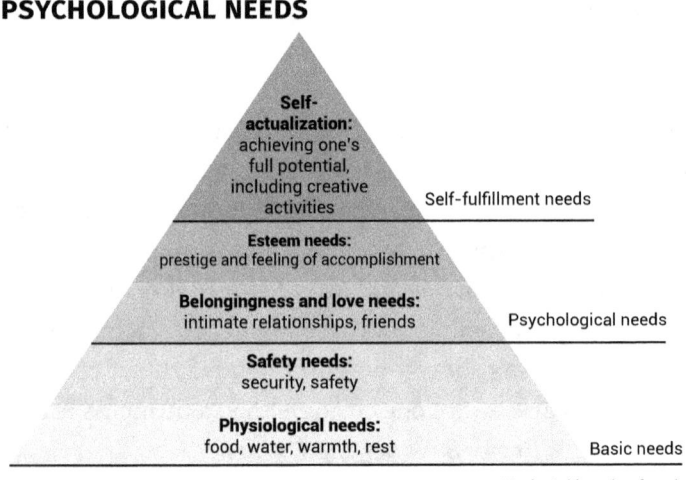

Maslow's Hierarchy of Needs (Poston, 2009)

As society improves, we yearn more and more for our psychological needs to be satisfied. Looking at Maslow's hierarchy of needs, the more the lower end of the pyramid is achieved, the more you need to fulfill the higher ones, which dabbles around belonging, esteem, and self-actualization. The bottom end of the pyramid must be fulfilled before any of the higher portions of the pyramid can be satisfied.

The higher people are on this pyramid, the higher the possibility for the individual to achieve their greatest potential. As a leader, you should help foster this growth. It is your responsibility to make each member of your team flourish in their work life and in their real life. Leadership involves having people become their better selves and it is up to you to help them fulfill this.

Have a plan to address the "pyramid of needs" all employees have—from physical, to mental and finally relational needs—so all levels are sustained.

ACCENTURE, 2020

Psychological safety is where you as a leader will need your emotional intelligence most. In order for people to thrive in the virtual environment that is different from the conventional office environment, you need to set up surroundings where all the members feel safe. It is as simple as giving them the space to work and trusting they will do what needs to be done.

Working from home often gives one a mental image of a lazy worker in their pajamas not doing their job, when in fact people *are* doing their jobs. It also requires understanding that more emergencies may arise in their household. As their leader, you must trust they will do their work at a time that is convenient and within the allotted time frame.

A leader's ability to address people's physical, mental and relational needs is the foundation of trust for their workforce. While all of these needs have equal importance, there is an order in which they make the biggest difference, starting at the base of the pyramid.

ACCENTURE, 2020

Understanding is needed for everyone to thrive in a virtual environment. You no longer have the standardized view that an office can provide. Instead, you end up viewing a kitchen, bedroom, patio, or a picture background. One needs to understand and look at things through the other person's lens. Some may be lucky enough to have a home office and some may not be able to afford one.

You need to understand that not everyone can turn on their cameras. They may not want to show their background—yes, I know, professionalism. Provide turning on cameras as an option and explain to them the benefits of doing so. You can give them multiple options. You can require a thumbnail for their profile, so when you have a conference, at least you can see faces and not blank screens. You can also ask the team members to add in a fake background. Others who are not as fortunate need to turn it off because of necessity rather than preference. Gone is the extreme professional structure of the office and in its place is the freer environment of working from home.

Although you should keep cameras as an option, depending on the situation you have, there might be times when it may be necessary, especially during important conversations, to ask people to turn on their cameras. Payton Lynch, author of *Rise from the Ashes* and a product manager at

The Walt Disney Company working on the Disney Cruise Line Navigator app, found it sometimes necessary to ask people to turn on their cameras. Payton may work with teams as large as fifty spanning from "Orlando, all the way to Colombia to India to everywhere [and they] often have many different [opinions]."

Payton and her team were working on a feature, and they were at a point in a project where they had to make a decision on something: "One group of people were in this side of the camp about it. And [they] had another group of people very passionate about the other side of it." So Payton, to the best of her ability, decided to ask people to turn on their cameras since the topic of discussion was an important one, although she does not "usually ask [people] to turn on their cameras, because [she] knows that everyone has different comfort levels." She said people have kids, dogs, and other distractors. However, she knows that "for [her team] to have this discussion [they] all had to be locking eyes with one another as much as possible." They did have that discussion but "in another call later, where the conversation did escalate. [She] shut [Zoom] down." You can feel the importance of the meeting, so at times like these, it may be necessary to have cameras on. Payton said it is best to inform the team beforehand if cameras will be required during the meeting, if possible. This is one struggle of working virtually.

Part of developing trust is being able to share emotion-laden situations without being criticized. Affect-based trust can be fostered by listening to team member's problems or providing useful information. McAllister found that those who had increased "affect-based" trust with their leader also reported higher levels of leadership effectiveness. Affect-based trust is rooted in the reciprocation of interpersonal concern and care (McAllister, 1995).

In some ways, working from home gives you a broader glimpse of an individual's life. Suddenly, you will learn they have kids without asking them after hearing kids screaming and talking in the background during your meeting. You will know the color of their walls, how they decorate their Christmas trees, and so on.

In a way, the struggles everyone encounters when working from home gives some sort of camaraderie. There is greater understanding that everyone is bound to have similar issues, such as pets parading themselves during an interview.

Once when I was in a virtual meeting, I had my camera on. I thought I turned it off when my brother came into the room. I forgot to turn it off and my brother was in the camera shirtless. For others who saw it, it might be hilarious. However, for the person who had this type of situation happen to them, it is embarrassing. In some ways working virtually may provide some accidental visibility to one's life.

Working virtually allows a more open and transparent discussion during meetings. Trust is hard to build in a virtual environment where limited body language exists and there is limited exposure to each other. Affect-based trust allows team members to connect with each other and are more welcoming to compromise and share information.

Emotional Intelligence will result in higher levels of team trust. Team trust facilitates constructive and collaborative group interactions, which positively affects team performance.

MELITA PRATI. CEASAR DOUGLAS. GERALD R. FERRIS. ANTHONY P. AMMETER AND M. RONALD BUCKLEY, 2003

The stress 2020 brought upon people made them more flexible and placed less pressure on everyone. Previously people in the office would wear suits and ties. Now you would see coworkers in their comfortable clothes. Gone were the work-centric views from the Boomer Generation; now we're welcoming the more lenient way of working. This is speeding up the pace of accepting the artist type of lifestyle.

The same goes for leading a team. You need to know what your team needs. A virtual environment is different from a face-to-face environment. A virtual leader must develop a robust emotional intelligence. As a leader, you are the person responsible for the people. This may include providing your team the support they may need. You need to be able to build an environment that provides psychological safety and promotes collaboration and productivity.

CHAPTER 3

IMPLEMENTING THE SMART HEART

WAYS TO IMPROVE YOUR EMOTIONAL INTELLIGENCE:

BE A LISTENER. USE ACTIVE LISTENING.
I had a roommate in college who was quiet. Most of the time, she just listened to me talk. When my birthday came, she gave me a stuffed Pooh Bear and a Pooh Bear-themed birthday card. I really appreciated it, knowing that she was listening. She was able to connect with me and gain my respect.

These days, when my team gathers to receive the updates at the end of the day, I give them the time to interact with each other. I tell them, "This is your time, feel free to talk to each other," and turn myself on mute to give them more time to speak or converse with them. Sometimes I place myself on mute at this point as to allow others to say their piece. If no one says anything, I prod the individuals in the team by asking them open-ended questions.

When you want to know about the other person, communication will be about them, not you. The best way to know the other person is to listen to what they say.

By giving my team time to talk and for me only to listen, I am gaining insights of who they are and what they are currently doing. I can connect with the team members better by connecting with them based on their interests.

Instead of thinking about what to say next, listen and understand what the other person is telling you.

REMEMBER NAMES AND USE THEM

Make others feel important; the best way to do that is by saying their name. This works well in a virtual environment. You can get people's attention by using their names. There is power in a name. It creates respect and recognition.

Back in summer 2016 I worked as a sales associate at Talbots. We all have those days when we are in a slump, maybe a bit drowsy at work. That afternoon, I was no longer my perky self, and I had a customer who came to me asking my name. When she asked for my name, I suddenly felt like a bucket of cold water was poured on me and I was alert and awake. By asking my name, she got my attention:

"Good afternoon. Anything I can help you with today?"

She replied, "Hi, I wanted to check the size for this shirt."

"I can do that for you," I responded and turned around to search for what she wanted.

She asked, "Wait, what's your name?" I gave her my name. I was sleepy that day, but once she asked for my name, I became alert and was more ready to assist.

People have always identified with their name; it is part of their being. Remember names and use them as another hook to connect with the person.

SHOW RESPECT FOR OTHER PEOPLE'S OPINIONS

So how do you facilitate conversations where opinions differ? Sometimes we get too passionate about the topic that we lose our heads when someone says something different than what we want to hear. So, I say, start with cooling off your head first, take a step back to see the information in a broader scope.

What I usually tend to do to gain further understanding of what someone says is I rephrase what they said in my own words and end with, "Is that what you meant?" or "Did I get it right?" By retelling what they just said, you show them you were listening and processing the information. After they give me a "yes" to indicate that that is what they said, I usually say, "Hmmm, that is a very interesting way to see things" or "That is very interesting." And, if there are other people in the room that needs to say their piece, I then move to them and ask them, "How about you [NAME OF THE PERSON], what do you think?"

After listening to everyone's opinion, I usually group similarities and differences. Stating what I just heard, I say, "Okay, I heard this and this," then state, "It seems to me that we should come to a middle ground here" or "We need to choose one or the other." Have a discussion of the advantages and disadvantages, then vote from there.

Oddly enough, the more you listen to other people's opinions, the more open they are to yours as well. Same goes with influence. If you allow people to influence you first, they will be more than welcome to what you tell them. It is part of the reciprocation, if people know they are being heard and understood, they will feel good and reciprocate those feelings.

Derek Gaunt, former hostage negotiator and award-winning author of *Ego, Authority, Failure,* said:

> *Approach interactions with everybody with the mindset of it not being about you. Let it be about them, before you jump into your goals and objectives. Allow others the chance to influence you, and as soon as you subordinate yourself to whomever you're in there interacting with, the quicker they are to reciprocate that in the conversation, the interaction is going to go a lot smoother.*
>
> DEREK GAUNT (GAUNT, 2020)

People like to be heard. If you listen, people are more willing to listen to you as well. Never dismiss what people say. It might just be as simple as an "uh-uh" reply or a few follow-up questions—people will appreciate that you were listening to them.

For Derek, whether in your professional or personal life, "One of the most powerful aspects of empathy is it encourages reciprocity." Reciprocity is part of the communication system; it does not have to be words it can be facial expression or body movements. In a virtual space in which people sometimes turn off their cameras, the only clue you may have is the tone of their voice (Gaunt, 2020).

At least as a leader, especially if you are going to have a heart-to-heart talk with a team member, ensure that you have the camera turned on on your end. Any way you can convey communication visually or through auditory will allow them to connect with you better.

EMPATHIZE
Understand what the other individual is going through. By empathizing with another individual, you are creating another deeper level of understanding towards their situation.

I interviewed Christopher Tam, senior director at Hilton Honors risk management, about his virtual leadership experience. This is a story he shared about what happened in his interview.

> *One time, I was interviewing someone, and the person actually stopped the interview to feed their pet bird. The person shut off the camera and came back a few minutes after. It is a little unprofessional, but at the same time, I think, you know, people have to recognize we're in the middle of a pandemic. Everybody's working from home. Everybody's under a lot of stress so I think that has changed the expectations of what's acceptable a little bit.*
>
> CHRISTOPHER TAM, SENIOR DIRECTOR AT
> HILTON HONORS RISK MANAGEMENT

Christopher used his EI and empathized with the individual in the context they were in. There should still be a level of professionalism and the workplace should not be treated like an anarchic environment. Professionalism, however, may need to be toned down compared to when people are in their offices. The virtual environment has a different work dynamic that may allow more business casual style with extra leniency ingrained into its culture.

Why is empathy so important in any kind of crisis or critical or challenging situation that we find ourselves?

> *Empathy is important because people love to have other people understand what they're going through. [For someone to] understand what the lay of the land looks like from their perspective. There are some studies that say there was a biological need to reach out for support.*
>
> DEREK GAUNT (GAUNT, 2020)

Practicing tactical empathy allows the listener to acknowledge the situation without being biased. It is having a bird's eye view, so you see and know what it is going on and at the same time can keep your feelings in check before responding to the situation.

Derek uses what he calls tactical empathy: "We call it tactical empathy, because it is a deliberate attempt on our part, to not only recognize the perspective of the other side, but to articulate that recognition." He does not mention empathy as walking in someone's shoes but more so looking at it through their point of view. "You'll never hear me say you need to walk in another person's shoes, that's tantamount to feeling what they feel. You don't need to feel what they feel to be empathetic. So instead of thinking of it as walking through another's shoes, think of it as looking through another's eyes." Tactical empathy means you're doing it deliberately to demonstrate your understanding (Gaunt, 2020). In a way, tactical empathy is understanding what the person is going through and still having the objective mind to view the multiple perspectives that surround the subject in question.

PRAISE THE BEHAVIORS YOU WANT TO BE RETAINED
In a virtual environment where people can run amok, praising one team member for good behavior allows others to see the actions desired and what to emulate. Praising the results may reinforce people to try to achieve the same type of result. For the behaviors you want to encourage, praise those individuals for doing the correct action. Practice this in moderation. If you overly praise, it may come off as being pretentious.

You should instead appreciate the behaviors that produced the result. For example, when my team members find a great information that is helpful and shares it with the team, I would tell them, "Love the creativity" or "Great observation." The best way to praise behaviors publicly is doing a shout-out.

Shout-outs are usually short announcements in which you tag the person you are praising and tell everybody that they did a great job with the specific scenario of what happened. I send shout-outs to my team Slack channel. The place where your team spends the most of its time communicating is the best place to send a shout-out; for example, if that place is group chats, I suggest sending shout-outs on that page.

USE EMOJIS OR GIFS

Emojis can enhance communication and social relationships. Emojis are supplementary aids and not a substitute for text. Refer to the communication chapter where I explain the in-depth value of emojis. GIFs, for example, create another form of interaction with others. With a picture or an emoji, you only see a cartoon of a dancing person not in motion; however, with GIFs you can see it in motion.

Tara Clements, a corporate systems lead project manager and my previous supervisor, added, "GIFs also lighten the overall mood and let your team know that while the work they are doing is important, it can still be a lighthearted environment," which is true.

Stan Murzyn, a sales executive at Mpathic and my other previous supervisor said GIFs are "the best way to communicate [his] personal energy via text."

GIFs and emojis serve as another way to connect with others. Software is really moving toward trying to capture as many human elements as possible, such as facial expression and movement.

Emojis can become conversation starters. One of my team members actually decided we needed to have our own specialized emojis and he started giving people assigned emojis.

Jake: "Winter should get the Easter stone, it fits you, Winter. Yeah, I think that one's for you."

Winter: "Yup, that's mine."

Jake: "Now, Mary what should be your emoji?"

Me: **Uses face with sunglasses emoji to react to a message**

Jake: "Now that's going to be your emoji, Mary."

An interview by Virtual not Distant Ltd with Rowena Hennigan and Sandra Thompson, from RISE Emotional Intelligence, touched the topic of emojis. Sandra said, "People don't mind talking about emotions. They just don't know how to. If they have something like an emoji or a card that has a word on it that describes an emotion, it gets the conversation going, and that's when you get to a much deeper creative conversation and a much stronger relationship." Sometimes visual tools like emojis allow an individual to express their emotions better (Virtual not Distant, 2020).

Rowena said she and Sandra had a conversation on LinkedIn where they "were looking at the different visual communications and visual cues from established remote teams and some of them use emojis and visuals. And [they] can refer to Lizette Sutherland's visual cue, or refer to emoji development which happens in specific remote teams in terms of response. They have their own little lingo in terms of approval. Some teams visual works well as a way of embedding or expressing but also reflecting their team culture if it has been customized in some way." Emojis can have multiple functionalities. In terms of team culture, they can serve as an "internal lingo" that builds understanding among all involve and, in a way, creates a community for those who know the meaning (Virtual not Distant, 2020).

In our company, the internal lingo emoji is the shrimp emoji.

No one knows how the shrimp emoji came about. Rumor has it that some team member accidentally used the shrimp emoji to reply, and the rest followed suit. What we all know, though, is that it is running rampant in the channels on our company's Slack. Random shrimp emojis have been added and are constantly being used for anything.

The shrimp emoji is such a part of the company culture, when my former supervisor, Tara Clements, first joined the company, she asked, "Why is there a shrimp emoji everywhere?" I thought that was interesting because something so small can be so easily recognizable and shared, becoming a common usage to anyone in the company. Something that all of us, no matter the position, share: a culture being cultivated by the shrimp emoji.

Virtual culture has a way of taking a life of its own. In this case, emojis that are often used in tools such as Slack may very well be a conversation starter. You will probably know if the person worked in my company if they know the shrimp emoji culture.

Culture is a great way to have the team be at ease. It gives them a story to share and helps build relationships.

Tara was the person from whom I learned to use emojis. I saw her using random food emojis when people said they were going to lunch. I soon decided to implement that on my team. It took a bit of time, about a week or two, before my team started picking the same habit as well. Sometimes, when we have a question of the day like "What's your favorite vegetable?" The emojis for lunch that day would all be vegetables. Someone even chose their own lunch emoji; for any person taking lunch she would use an avocado emoji, and another chose a chicken drumstick.

One of the pregnant team members mentioned she likes to drink orange juice and eat carrots nonstop. When she said she was going to lunch, another team member actually gave her a carrot emoji. She thanked the team member and the conversation carried on a bit longer throughout the week about her fondness of orange juice, carrots, and her pregnancy. Small conversations add up and become relationship-building blocks.

Emotional intelligence allows the individual to perform better and helps others be productive. As the bond within the team strengthens, they are more willing to collaborate with each other. The virtual workspace provides a different dynamic of openness and transparency, making people engage with each other in a more personalized way.

Knowing yourself allows you to understand your emotions and control them in a way that best fits situations. Self-regulation allows an individual to maintain a level head, even in times of change and unfavorable conditions. Having social awareness allows you to understand what is going on around you, including how to interact with others.

Emotional intelligence allows an individual to understand others. Being an emotionally intelligent leader will allow you to build a better team that is welcoming, accepting of one another, and high performing. As people collaborate in a unified manner, goals will be achieved.

EI and trust go hand in hand. You will need your EI to foster trust.

KNOWLEDGE NUGGETS:
- **Be A Listener. Use Active Listening.** Listen not to reply; listen with the intention to understand.
- **Remember Names and Use Them.** Names are valuable and connect the individuals to themselves.
- **Show Respect for Other People's Opinions.** Allow reciprocation and understanding by respecting other people's opinions.
- **Empathize.** See the situation through the other person's lens.
- **Praise the Behaviors You Want to Be Retained.** Use praise to boost the individual's confidence and let the team member know the best practices.
- **Use Emojis or GIFs.** Emojis and GIFs can be used as tools to help build the virtual environment culture.

CHAPTER 4

RECIPROCITY OF TRUST

Trust is a foundation of a strong relationship, may it be personal or professional. It is strong enough to be able to affect an organization's overall well-being.

> *There is a strong connection between a high-trust culture and business success. In fact, the connection is so strong that it can reasonably be argued that strategy-minded leaders, who care deeply about the financial well-being of their business, should make building a high-trust culture a top priority.*
>
> JESSICA ROHMAN, MANAGEMENT CONSULTANT AT BLUE BEYOND CONSULTING (ROHMAN, 2021)

Trust is one of the most important things in leadership. Without trust, you cannot influence people. You can boss them around, which will work for short term leadership but not in the long term. Trust takes time to build and strengthen.

One thing I learned from nursing school is the very first thing that a nurse establishes with a patient is their trust. The initial moment the nurse interacts with the patient is the moment they start building rapport with them. Trust is highly valuable in the health care field; without the patient's trust, one will have a great difficulty establishing cooperation in their treatment process. It would be hard for a nurse to assist the patients if the patients do not cooperate with them—trust is key to that.

The best way to begin and gain trust from another person is through authenticity. Nurses build rapport with patients by introducing themselves and their role, following through with what they say they will do, as well as explaining the steps of what the nurse does and why.

After the initial introduction with your team members, the best way to establish trust is authenticity. Let them know what you are doing and why. This will also help with clarity.

The nurses' situation also applies to teams, may they be face-to-face or virtual teams. A leader will have a hard time if the team members do not cooperate. Trust fosters cooperation and collaboration.

Mutual trust is needed for the team to function properly; no micromanagement is necessary since virtual teams tend to be a more independent work situation. Tesluk and Gerstner found successful leaders do not engage in micromanagement but instead provide clear objectives that allow them to establish mutual trust and bring about stronger team relationships (Derosa, Donald, Hantula, Kock, and D'Arcy, 2004).

The leader is there to clarify the goal and see the progress of the results. In the book *The One Minute Manager* by Kenneth

Blanchard and Spencer Johnson, the one-minute manager focuses on the outcome while giving more freedom and control to the team member about the how-to's of the job and providing them direction when necessary. This decreases the stress for both the manager and the team members (Blanchard and Johnson, 1982). Teach the team first how to do it and allow them to do their job. Trust is needed so the leader does not micromanage the team. Trust that even if the team is not supervised, it will do its job. I am not saying to blindly trust people, but allow others to showcase themselves and their capabilities. Knowing when to trust and when to evaluate is a key skill that needs to be practiced appropriately.

According to the research in *Dynamic Nature of Trust in Virtual Teams*, "The lack of a shared work history, coupled with the absence of face-to-face communication, makes it harder for virtual team members to gather information and evaluate one another's behaviors." It is also the absence of face-to face interaction that creates further psychological and physical distance between members of the team (Kanawattanachai and Yoo, 2002).

One of the foundational pillars that must be built in a team, whether virtual or not, is trust. As Stephen M.R. Covey would say, *trust* "is the one thing that if you remove will destroy the most powerful government and successful business, but if developed and leveraged has the potential to create unparalleled success and prosperity in any dimension of life. Trust is the one thing that changes everything." Stephen Covey is the co-founder and CEO of CoveyLink Worldwide. He received MBA from Harvard Business school and is renowned because of his book *The Speed of Trust* (Covey, 2008).

In Stephen Covey's talk on the speed of trust, he gave an example of when he was a young boy at age seven. His dad had given him the task of keeping their family's lawn green and clean. At first, Stephen failed to take care of the lawn. Instead of taking the job himself, his father told Stephen one day that they should take a walk and see the lawn. Stephen was embarrassed by his shortcomings; he told his dad that it was hard (Covey, 2016).

His dad then replied, "What's so hard, son? You have not done anything yet" (Covey, 2016).

Stephen asked his dad if he would help show him how to take care of the yard, to which he said yes; he had the time that afternoon. Stephen gave one garbage bag to his dad and got one for himself. They spent the rest of the afternoon cleaning up the lawn. It was at that moment that Stephen took on the responsibility of keeping their lawn green and clean. Stephen felt he was trusted and did not want to let his dad down, and it inspired him. It brought out the best in him. From then on, he rose to the occasion to do the job (Covey, 2016).

Stephen's experience can reflect that of a work environment. At first, if the team member fails in producing the results needed, the leader should not reduce the responsibility. Instead, the leader should show how the job is done and leave it for the team member to follow through with the task at hand.

The spatial and temporal distances in virtual situations demand that leaders focus more on results and performance. Once the team member feels trusted, they will be inspired to take on the job better. Ken Blanchard and Spencer Johnson said, "People who feel good about themselves produce good results," and rightfully so (Blanchard and Johnson, 1982). By placing people in a good headspace, they can show more of their potential.

The significant difference that a conventional office and a virtual office is that you can barely see some co-workers. You can no longer see people working at their desk, so you have to trust that people are doing their job.

One of the causes why managers fail in leading a virtual team is the lack of trust. Studies show that a manager who does not trust the people in their care becomes overzealous and micromanaging.

If you feel trusted, you feel more responsible, and if you are responsible, you earn more trust. It's simple.
NUNO BALADIA, DOIST'S HEAD OF IOS (BALANDIA, 2021)

The lack of trust in any relationship causes productivity to decrease. It is hard for some managers to adjust to the virtual environment. An in-person setting allows easy access to your team members, whereas in a virtual environment, it is hard to monitor them and see reports.

Once a lack of trust invades a team, it further creates a decrease in the productivity cycle. The less trust there is, the more the manager micromanages the team project. In its 2016 global CEO survey, PwC reported 55 percent of CEOs think a lack of trust is a threat to their organization's growth (Zak, 2017).

In a virtual environment, trust is greatly needed. A leader can either do two things that may affect their work culture.
1. Introduce a virtual monitoring system.
2. Trust that the team members will do their job.

Trust and Leadership in Virtual Teamwork: A Media Naturalness Perspective pointed out, "No matter how complicated the next new technology may seem, it is still the human that is the most complex, flexible, and adaptive part of the system" (DeRosa, Hantula, Kock, and D'Arcy, 2004). Just think of how humans have come to evolve along the way, from fire to computer, and from working in an office to working remotely. We humans changed along with the world "to the extent that we can adapt communication technology to ourselves, we will, and to the extent, we cannot adopt the technology, we will adapt to it" (DeRosa, Hantula, Kock, and D'Arcy, 2004). So, as virtual leaders, we must mold the environment in favor to the people and use technology as aid.

Team building is also important in a virtual environment; team building fosters trust between team members. Building trust also requires good communication. According to Stephen, "To accelerate trust: clear your intent 'why' + signal your behavior, 'tell them what you are going to do' + You do what you say you do" (Stephen, 2018). Whenever I give performance feedback, I tell the team member the reason behind the feedback (intent). Before finishing the feedback meeting, I tell them I am going to submit the document and I will tag them in it so they can see (tell them what I am going to do), and lastly, do exactly what I told them to do. The transparency of the actions taken builds a deeper understanding and produces clarity.

A virtual leader's task will focus more on coaching and support, coaching in terms of getting the team clear on the operations. Support is providing all the necessary documentation distributed to the individual team members so they will have the resources they need to use to be successful with their job. Trust begets trust. As you trust them, they too will trust you. A leader who earns high trust among their team members has members that are more willing to go above and beyond what they are tasked to do.

> *If I had to pick the one thing to get right about any collaborative effort, I would choose trust. Yes, trust. More than incentives, technology, roles, missions, or structures, it is trust that makes collaboration really work. There can be collaboration without it, but it won't be very productive or sustainable in the long run.*
>
> LARRY PRUSAK, SENIOR ADVISOR AND FACULTY, AUTHOR OF *WORKING KNOWLEDGE* (PRUSAK, 2011)

CHAPTER 5

POWER OF TRUST

WAYS TO BUILD TRUST

INTRODUCE YOURSELF

Focus on communication improve trust levels not only in components directly connected to communication (openness and honesty, concern for stakeholders) but also in other components (identification, competence, fairness/reliability).

BENETYTĖ AND JATULIAVIČIENĖ, 2013

Do a one-on-one with your team member as soon as they are onboarded. Do not be a mysterious blob in their mind. Give them an image of you by actually taking time to do an introduction. When I first onboarded my team, I did a ten-minute introduction with them, a short introduction of myself, and then had them introduce themselves. And I encouraged them to share history they were willing to share and future things they might want me to help them with. I had a team member who mentioned in the introduction that he wanted to be promoted to a supervisor. Had I not done that, I would not have known his goal. He later did get promoted to become a supervisor; I was glad to see his growth in the company and the positive impact it brought to his career.

During my time with the company, I was onboarded in two teams. When I was first onboarded, my supervisor never did a one-on-one with me, because of her busy schedule. When I was switched to a different team, my supervisor, Stan Murzyn, reached out to do a ten-minute one-on-one with me. From him, I learned it is essential to do one-on-ones with all team members.

I started with a short introduction of myself, and he asked how he could help me. It felt good that he did that; it made him feel closer than some random person bossing me around. Similar to a nurse who can be involved with things that are personal to the patients, it is uncomfortable to be put in a position where you have to share some of your private matters to someone whom you just met. Introducing yourself is the first step in breaking the "stranger barrier."

Be intentional in creating relationships. Paul Zak, an American neuroeconomist, states, "When people more intentionally build social ties at work, their performance improves" (Zak, 2017). If you do not do a one-on-one intentionally, you can fall into the habit of just having a group chat with everyone.

> *So much of it is just really paying attention to be one on one with people. And a lot of times, social media can be more of a group thing. What I like to think of*

social media is like picture an iceberg. And that is, when you see people, you are only seeing the tip, and the whole person is underneath.

JEN MARR, FOUNDER OF INSPIRING COMFORT; MENTAL HEALTH THROUGH ANIMAL CONNECTIONS (MARR, 2020)

One-on-one is another way to better understand the individual.

Amid the social media hype, it has slowly become acceptable to be on your phone and be isolated in your room. Jen Marr mentioned it has become a crutch, mainly in that it produces a shallow understanding of the individual. We fail to dive deep and only have a superficial understanding of people around us. One-on-one meetings are an opportunity to "break through this awkwardness" (Marr, 2020). One-on-ones are a great way to get to know people more in depth.

KEEP YOUR WORD, FOLLOW THROUGH
Your words and deeds must match if you expect employees to trust in your leadership.

KEVIN KRUSE, FOUNDER AND CEO OF LEADX (CONANTLEADERSHIP, 2015)

Traci Baird is president and CEO of EngenderHealth, an international organization that works on sexual reproductive health and rights. Baird leads a team of almost four hundred employees around the world, thirty-five in the United States and the rest in sub-Saharan Africa and India. She has been working for twenty-five years for nonprofit international health.

When her team all went remote in March because of the coronavirus pandemic, it had three priorities. The first priority "is the health and safety of [its] staff. The second priority is to support [its] communities and the third priority is to make sure [it keeps] doing the good work that [it does]. And it's only because [it supports its] staff that [it] can do the work that [it does]." This is the first priority; without the people there is no organization, so take care of them well.

When one of the team members in the United States was diagnosed with COVID-19, Traci "got on Amazon and started sending care package stuff, [she] was too far away from that person to drop stuff off. [She] can order water bottles and cozy blankets and snack food." Traci kept her word; she said she would take care of her team and she did just that. Follow through with what you promised; people will remember what you said and what you did. The moment you lead a team is the moment you promise to take care of them. Follow through with your actions and let them know you care about them and that they matter.

My personal example of following through was creating an easier way to organize the information my team members needed to assist clients. My way of organizing information was creating folders in Slack to organize the information that was shared in multiple places throughout various Slack channels. My team told me it was very hard to find information on Slack. Granted, there were about five hundred individuals at that time exchanging information, making it hard to find the most relevant information for a particular situation. The communication system was so overloaded with information that it was hard to segregate the good ones from the duds.

That evening, I tried to think of a way to make it easier for the team members to find the right resources. So, I created an optimized folder system for people to access the information.

The next day, when I introduced it to the team members, they were happy, and most of them still use it frequently. My point is: I asked them what they were having problems with, they told me, and I solved it. When I first talked to my team, I told them my job was to serve them and help them be successful. I followed through on my word that my main purpose was to help them succeed.

BUILD AN ENVIRONMENT THAT FOSTERS SUCCESS

Trust is a multidimensional construct with both cognitive (e.g., competence, reliability, professionalism) and affective elements (e.g. caring, emotional connection to each other).

KANAWATTANACHAI AND YOO, 2002

One thing I did when I first built my team was get my resources together and build systems in the software we were using. The more competent you are, the easier it is for the individuals on your team to feel some sort of psychological safety. Having confidence that you know how to perform your job means you can take care of them.

According to the study on *Dynamic Nature of Trust in Virtual Teams*, a study that was done on MBA student virtual teams in six universities, discovered that "high-performing teams were able to continue to perform at a high level since trust among the team members facilitated the flow of knowledge and cooperation (Deutsch, 1958, Huemer et al., 1998) while reducing the level of uncertainty (Sorrentino et al., 1995)"

(Kanawattanachai and Yoo, 2002). The more informed and competent the team is, the more secure and comfortable they will feel at work.

Reliability increases trust. My organization was using Slack as a means of synchronous communication. On the first week I worked, I added automated systems into my team channel, for example scheduling meetings with links attached to them. Any daily reminders were also automated. The more organized the systems were, the more comfortable the staff members became. They no longer had to ask where the Zoom link was because at the meeting time Slack automatically sent them the link, and the team knew when to expect the link to pop up. The team members are now also very communicative with each other and share information freely.

High-performing teams not only quickly establish trust at the beginning, but also manage to maintain it at a high level throughout the project.

KANAWATTANACHAI AND YOO, 2002

BE TRANSPARENT

The experiment conducted by Paul Zak revealed that "having sense of higher purpose stimulates oxytocin production, as does trust. Trust and purpose then mutually reinforce each other, providing a mechanism for extended oxytocin release, which produces happiness" (Zak, 2017). Be transparent in your goals and show others the path that you are all taking as a team.

Authenticity, openness, or transparency helps with the release of the hormone oxytocin. One of the causes that inhibits its release is chronic stress. Around 40 percent of employees say they are informed about the goals and processes of the companies, and the lack of information creates stress. The higher the uncertainty, the greater the stress (Zak, 2017).

In a study conducted by IBM, over seventeen hundred CEOs in eighteen industries in 2012 found "companies that outperform their peers are 30 percent more likely to identify openness as a key influence on their organization," and these CEOs incorporate "openness, transparency and employee empowerment into their workplace cultures" (Rohman, 2016). Transparency allows others to understand and know you more. It provides an openness that makes it easier to reciprocate and nurture a relationship.
- Daily communication can help with this.
- Be direct and concise.
- Let the team know what events are going on in the organization.
- Be honest.

SHOW VULNERABILITY AND BE AUTHENTIC
Jim Whitehurst, CEO of open-source software maker Red Hat, has said, "I found that being very open about the things I did not know actually had the opposite effect than I would have thought. It helped me build credibility. Asking for help is effective because it taps into the natural human impulse to cooperate with others" (Zak, 2017).

When I got promoted, it was my first leadership role. I had been offered several leadership roles, but I had never accepted them because I thought I was not ready yet. When I did get promoted, I knew my responsibilities were expanded as

I took the approach from a self-centered to team-centered relationship. I was absolutely nervous on my first day. I did not have an experience leading such a large team or leading people who were twice or three times my age.

On my second day, I was introduced to my team. Not knowing what to do first, I just messaged them via Slack at the end of the day. I found out that if this were to continue, I would lose my team's trust because first, they had not seen me and secondly, they were also new. So the next day I had a Zoom call with them and asked them to please be patient and give me the time to adjust to the new role.

I did not have a lot of experience and wanted their cooperation in working with me. I delegated tasks to the senior members who were previously in a different team. It worked out well. It was very surprising. A lot of my team members ended up helping me, which made it possible for everyone to build a relationship right off the bat. I never pretended I knew what I was doing; I simply promised to do my best and followed through. Some of the people in my group were almost three times my age and they gave me some advice as well. People like a culture where they are seen and heard.

You can foster trust through a blameless culture. Etsy created a "blameless" culture to foster learning. This allows employees to talk about the issue and learn from it openly. They have an event called "Blameless Postmortems, in which the people involved in a situation, and those interested in learning about it, come together to discuss what happened and craft a plan for the future." A "blameless" culture provides psychological safety (Rohman, 2016).

If people feel safe, they are more understanding of mistakes and imperfections. Jen Marr said, "There's a great quote out there that says that, the common touch of humanity that gives the world true kinship, like true connection isn't happiness and joy, it's tough times and sorrow." The shared collective of understanding the struggles we all face and those difficult times are when the "deepest bonds of friendship are going to happen, and closest ties will be formed, because it's when we're most vulnerable. It's when we're most open to share." People bring down their walls and can freely approach each other (Marr, 2020).

ALLOW PEOPLE TO TAKE CHARGE OF THEIR WORK
> *Once employees have been trained, allow them, whenever possible, to manage people and execute projects in their own way. Being trusted to figure things out is a big motivator: A 2014 Citigroup and LinkedIn survey found nearly half of employees would give up a 20 percent raise for greater control over how they work.*
>
> PAUL J. ZAK, AMERICAN NEUROECONOMIST (ZAK, 2017)

Being trusted fosters trust. Empower the people in your care to trust themselves. The best way to encourage people to trust in themselves is to give them the autonomy to do their work. It is easy for a person who has good self-esteem to trust others. The pervasive thought of having someone breathing down their necks to check the results of their work causes the individual to be distracted.

There is an individual on my team who has a hard time making decisions, so I told her I trusted her. Now, I am not implying that you should practice blind trust. I have observed her, and she is well informed and is constantly asking how to interpret the updates given during the team meeting. By telling her I trust her, I am empowering her to do her job. Obviously, I still monitor results at the end every now and then. So far, trusting her hasn't backfired. Instead, it made her more independent in doing her work.

Autonomy also promotes innovation, because different people try different approaches.
PAUL ZAK, AMERICAN NEUROECONOMIST (ZAK, 2017)

ESTABLISH CREDIBILITY

Credibility is developed when managers and leaders are competent, consistently keep their word, and share information with employees as openly as possible. The more committed leaders are to honoring their word, the more trust employees will place in their ability to lead.
JESSICA ROHMAN, MANAGEMENT CONSULTANT AT
BLUE BEYOND CONSULTING (ROHMAN, 2016)

Credibility can affect trust. Team members will not feel you are trustworthy and will be able to take care of them if you do not show credibility. It is hard to trust an incompetent leader; people will lose trust in you, their team members, and the company.

In a virtual environment, you will need to show you are also capable of resolving technological issues. It may be as simple as choosing the right tools that can help your team with their day-to-day tasks. Virtual teams "rely heavily on task-based trust, which is the belief that team members will do their job, DeRosa said" (Hirsch, 2019). Team members can obtain the trust of their co-workers by being committed, responsible, and overall responsive (Hirsch, 2019).

I often see this in a lot of work environments. If a leader does not know what they are doing, it is harder for them to gain traction in leading others. One of my team members was able to build his credibility right from the get-go. He trained a lot of the team members and resolved some of their issues, from technical issues to any other work-related issues. I often hear people praise him. Other team members come to him when they needed help. Just by knowing how to do things, he was able to create a name for himself and a lot of team members trust him for the right information.

Follow through on things you say and lead by example. If you tell them to do it a certain way, do it that way as well.

Trust increases engagement. Rapport with each individual is the bridge that allows everyone to build a collaborative environment. Trust is the heart of influence. Without trust, you cannot genuinely influence others; you can trick them, but you cannot influence them.

A trustworthy leader earns the loyalty of the team, and they will more likely allow you to lead them and follow your outrageous ideas. One of the questions that managers have is how to manage their team. There might be a great temptation to micromanage your team. Maybe part of micromanaging is thinking people will not do the job as well as a manager, so they take it upon themselves to do the job. Instead of micromanaging, give them the ability to show you what they can do.

Give your team your trust and encourage them to reach the results needed to be productive; most employees wishe to do well, believe in them.

KNOWLEDGE NUGGETS:
- **Introduce Yourself.** Make it so that they know you, even though it is hard to get to know people in a virtual work environment.
- **Keep Your Word, Follow Through.** Say it and do it.
- **Build an Environment that Fosters Success.** Make it easy for individuals to do their work. Provide a place that is safe.
- **Be Transparent.** Be clear on what path your team is going to take.
- **Show Vulnerability and Be Authentic.** Share some of your struggles and do not pretend to be perfect; be human.
- **Allow People to Take Charge of Their Work.** Allow people to do their work and do not do their work. Give them the chance to show their potential.
- **Establish Credibility.** Perform your job and do it well.

CHAPTER 6

SETTING MARGINS

Clarity of vision creates clarity of priorities.
JOHN MAXWELL, AMERICAN AUTHOR,
SPEAKER, AND PASTOR

The lack of clarity should drive one to keep moving; since things are unclear, there is an urge to clarify. Imagine a team of workers. If the team does not know what they are tasked to do and what their roles are, it is very unlikely they will accomplish anything.

It's like having all the parts of the machine without knowing which button to press for it to continue functioning. Imagine a clock. A clock is a machine that is a sum of its parts: the hour hand, the minute hand, the battery container, and the battery. If the hour hand and the minute hand were switched, the clock would give you the wrong time. It is the same with the team: if roles are not clarified, the team may not function properly as one cohesive unit. If something is unclear when you notice it as a leader, you will need to clarify the situation.

Why is clarity important for remote teams? For some, working remotely is a new situation for them. If you were placed in a random room without any instructions whatsoever, wouldn't you be confused as to what is going on? Well, for some individuals, that is the case with virtual work.

Remote work is not only a change; it is also a new form of work. If you introduce something new, it is best to be clear on what the new rules and regulations are, what expectations to follow, and perhaps how the changes in environment somewhat alter the job description.

Clarity brings forth a common goal for a team to achieve. Providing the vision and directing the team toward that vision help drive the team to a common goal they fully execute on. By having clarity, you will be able to solve problems easily.

IDENTIFY → FOCUS → EXECUTE

When you identify your problem, you can isolate the discussion on how to execute your solution. I love this tactic; this is how I am able to solve many issues. To achieve success in any issues, you must first gain clarity, which will allow you to identify the issue. Once you have identified the issue, focus on finding ways to solve it, and lastly execute; execution is where decisiveness matters most.

Often I see leaders being so afraid to make the wrong call that they get stuck in the analysis paralysis. Guess what: your indecisiveness will cause you and your team more stress and inefficiency. I am not saying you should outright decide immediately and be careless. Do not do that either. You will know when enough planning is enough.

To be successful in solving the issue, execution is the next action that is needed. Clarity, however, will be the first step. If you do not decide, that is the moment you have made your decision; you have given the person next to you the power to decide. I do not think this is bad. I am fine allowing others to make the decision. The hard part comes when you end up blaming the other person about their decision when you did not give one yourself.

In a virtual work environment, you have to attain clarity on three subjects:
1. Role clarity
2. Clarity of work boundaries
3. Clarity of vision

Approximately around 49 percent of workers do not know what is expected from them in the areas revolving around "availability, work productivity standards, and working hours (Wrike, 2021)." I give them the specifics and make it measurable. For example, I am expecting you to be available from X time until Y time.

Clarify what boundaries you want to establish that include what role someone has, how they can help the team, what is expected of them, and what constraints they need to understand. In the new virtual environment people need to understand more what their role is in the job ecosystem so they can function well as an individual part and in the collective group. The more people know what you want from them, the more precise and accurately they can deliver what you want.

ROLE CLARITY

No one wants to work with a leader who is unable to deliver their message clearly. For example, if you are unable to communicate your vision properly, your team will struggle and be disorganized.

The project I was in was a temporary contract that often would be extended on an as needed basis. As we were heading closer to the end of the year and renewal of the contract, the leadership mentioned they would be looking for the "cream of the crop agents," the high-performing agents for any leadership potential.

The afternoon when I had my meeting with my agents, I told them they should try to place their best foot forward.

Another agent asked how they could perform better.

I told them, "Well, you can try to participate more on answering team member questions on Slack."

Another agent intervened and replied, "How can we do that when most of our time is spent answering phone calls? We do not have time to answer other people."

To that I replied, "You can just answer if you have time."

She replied, "I do not understand why you ask that from us when we are already busy enough."

The conversation went on and on until I finally understood what the agent was talking about. The agent thought it was required of her to answer questions. However, what I meant was for them to stand out and get promoted, they needed to do other things besides answer the phones. They needed to show teamwork and so on.

Part of the conversation touched the topic of what their job description was. If they did not know what their role entailed, they would not know what going beyond that role means. I had to tell them again what the expectations were for their current position and what they could do to stand out. It was my fault for not being clear with the agents, which caused quite a debacle.

I was still a bit unclear as to why people were having a hard time with what I said about "placing their best foot forward." That night I thought hard and long as to what prompted the team members to have such a reaction. Then it clicked, and, like a switch had been turned on, I realized my team members did not know how to place their best foot forward.

We were in a virtual space; the team had never been in such an environment before. They did not know how to move around this new environment. I devised a plan on what I could tell my team members. The next few days, I tried to figure out ways in which it would not hinder their current job and contribute to the overall company vision. I thought, *Why not have them participate in building the culture?*

At the end of the day, the team has an hour where phones are off. I took my agents and had a one-on-one session with them.

I clarified my vision to them once again. "My main purpose as your team lead is to place you in a position where you can thrive and you can grow. If you want to get promoted, there are ways you can showcase yourself so that you can be in the field of vision of the leadership team as well as HR."

I told them that in this new virtual environment where the watercooler conversations are no longer occurring, in order for you to get noticed, you have to be intentional and purposeful in your ways. "I want the leadership team to notice you, I want you to get out there and be seen. We have several channels where you can post content. Similar to how social media works, you have to gain followers, so you need to become a content creator. Post in the positivity channel, random channel, or question of the day channel. Engage with other teams and place yourself in the spotlight."

What made this actionable for my team members is I was clear in my directions of what they could be doing to showcase their growth and productivity within the company. It was evident that if they wanted a promotion, they needed to show initiative. Clarity of what needs to be done created a proactive mindset and triggered actions.

Clarify your team's roles. Create an accountability chart that shows what each position in the company is accountable for. By knowing who is accountable for what results, everyone will be able to identify the role that they play in the company ecosystem.

According to Darleen DeRosa, a managing partner at OnPoint Consulting, a leadership assessment company based in New York City, "leaders have to make it clear to team members that they are responsible for their own actions and the impact their actions have on the rest of the team" (Hirsch, 2019). Telling your team who is accountable for which tasks will clarify the roles.

Part of what managers are afraid of when going virtual is the lack of control and view to the people in their care. You need to be clear and establish rules and regulations.

For the work we do, one of the primary data that helps the project be successful is hours and scheduling. For this particular issue, I have established with the team members some rules in terms of the schedule. Unless it is an emergency, they need to let me know what days they will be leaving beforehand. If they know the exact date and duration they need off, I told them to submit their time-off requests so I could approve them. And for the team responsible for analyzing the data hours, they can have access to this new information.

There are also times when everyone is required to be logged in into their systems. Consequently, when they join the team, I inform the new team member about the time blocks they are required to be logged in for. This is part of setting up expectation and providing clarity. In the beginning, when I just told them the time I was doing my count of how many people were logged in, a lot of the members kept forgetting. By giving them the range of time that I needed the team to be signed on, they were able to fulfill what was asked of them. By being clear on my expectations, everyone is able to do their job properly.

One of my team members was having a hard time producing the needed statistics. When I had a one-on-one talk with her, I was able to understand that she had a confusion about what she needed to do. A simple clarification on her job role helped her excel, and now she is one of my best performers.

Make part of the feedback on roles personalized. Thomas Sullivan, leadership coach and Hult Ashridge professor of leadership skills, has twenty years of experience leading and implementing his teachings. He noticed how the virtual environment causes boundaries to be blurred, especially ones "around responsibilities" (Sullivan, 2019). A shift in the work environment will throw off people's routines, and this includes confusion about their existing role.

Thomas said to "make sure specific actions are assigned to everyone involved after each meeting, and a blanket announcement to everyone may lead to a bystander effect, wherein the absence of clear direction, everyone relies on someone else to take action" (Sullivan, 2019). Try telling a group of people you need a specific task to be done without assigning it to a specific person. You will notice that the task will not get done. Clarify what the task is and who is responsible for them—make the line visible.

CLARITY OF BOUNDARIES

In the 2021 *State of Remote Work* report by Buffer, the biggest struggle with working remotely is unplugging after work (Buffer, 2021). Michelle LaBrosse, CEO and founder of Cheetah Learning and author of *Cheetah Project Management* and *Cheetah Negotiations*, said, "Set some boundaries for yourself, and let your team know when you're not available. If you're on a family vacation, give people plenty of notice, and let them know the time period when you are not available. Empower people when you are unavailable" (LaBrosse, 2010).

Part of setting the boundary is having a healthy level of trust. Trust your team can do their job and empower them. Delineating the proper time of communication among team members provides transparency and clarity.

One of the hot topics around virtual work is worker burnout. To reduce the stress, you should be cognizant of people's time and when you are calling them for work. I have no issue with people working above and beyond what is required of them; what I do care about are overworking and burnout. In the context of a virtual environment, communication becomes easily accessible to a point that others break through the barriers of professionalism.

Mark Bundang was reading an article and he said:

> This article had me at '…this can lead to sitting at dinner while your daughter tells a story about her day, but instead of hearing her you're wondering whether an email from your boss came through.' I am guilty… [it's] important to set boundaries, specifically around connectivity after hours. Boundaries are even more blurry these days during the pandemic and WFH.
>
> MARK BUNDANG, STRATEGIST, CHANGE, AND PROJECT MANAGER (BUNDANG, 2021)

We have been wearing the overwork medal for a long time, speaking to each other as if it's a prize to be won. It is not nice nor cool to be overworked, so take off that medal and stomp on it. Make sure you are not overworked, avoid it like a plague, and maintain a healthy life balance.

One of my teammates mentioned that "one thing [she] love about this job is that once the clock is off, we are done." Being a teacher previously before this job, part of the reason why she did a career shift is that "even during weekends you still think about work and never have an off day. It gets exhausting." Burnout happens pretty fast if the line is not set—so set it. I organize tasks so I do not contact the team about work after hours; after all, the leader sets the pace of the team.

Clarify when it should be appropriate to call each other when the clock is off. I found out a lot of people who work remote are constantly on working mode. One co-worker said she was clocked in from 7:00 a.m. up until 7:00 p.m. Other times, she catches herself still working after work hours. I'm not sure about you, but there are twenty-four hours in one day; she pretty much spends most of her day working, from the weekdays to the weekends. Burning the candle at both ends sure applies to her situation.

Being a hard worker is not an issue, however when habits are not checked and kept in moderation, it may cause issues such as burnout. Employees are not only workers; some are also full-time caregivers and part-time teachers for their children. Playing many roles in a day may eventually lead to burnout.

Expect the same thing with your team members. Stop blasting them with content information outside of work. I find it quite stressful when I am done for the day and wanting to relax, only to find myself being emailed about projects. I personally like to send people information early in the morning during workdays and not on Friday, Saturday, or Sunday, nor do I expect for them to be thinking about what I want them to do during their relaxation time. Give them the time to replenish their energy without your interfering and buzzing their phone nonstop.

Zoom fatigue is real. One of my coworkers commented, "It's because you have to constantly plaster on your work face." According to the ILO-Eurofound 2017 research report, "a study by the United Nations revealed that 41 percent of remote workers report high stress levels," while only 25 percent of the in-office report high stress levels, indicating that the "stress is directly related to aspects of the remote work environment" (Greene, 2020). In-office and remote have their own advantages and disadvantages. If workers are not careful, it may lead to stress that could have been prevented.

Owl Labs produces a yearly report to share how remote work can improve outcome for teams, employees, and organization. Owl Labs found that over 43 percent of remote workers were more "likely to exceed a forty-hour work week compared with non-remote workers" (Owl Labs, 2021). You have the opportunity to guide the team members to create a healthy working environment that is more conducive to productivity.

Allow people not to think of work constantly. People need time-off from work. Respect after working hours and allow individuals to do other activities besides work. This makes them more revitalized when they come to work the next day. Sometimes people need breathing time to clear the brain fog. Brain fog tends to delay the brain processing time. Busy does not always mean productive, which a lot of people unfortunately confuse. We need to move from working hard to working smart. Give the team space to breathe and they will feel much better. After all, absence makes the heart grow fonder.

Without focusing and getting to clarity you cannot lead. You cannot motivate. You cannot plan. You cannot communicate.
BOBB BIEHL, EXECUTIVE MENTOR AND AUTHOR

CLARITY OF VISION
When why is clear the how is easy.
ANONYMOUS

I have mentioned the huge issue our project was having was managing time. We are required to fulfill an amount of full-time hours per day. The workers in the project were promised flexibility on the employer side, and a mix of part-time and full-time workers filled the organization. Over time, it was getting hard to manage the issue. Fluctuations of people coming in and asking time off on the same day and the schedule were not aligning.

Christian "Chris" Koch, chairman, president, and CEO of Carlisle Companies Incorporated said:

> You must have access to the front-line workers and understand what matters to them and how the work

> *gets done. Without a clear understanding of where and how the business adds value, it's difficult to see how a leader can drive efficiencies and effectiveness through their team.*
>
> CHRISTIAN KOCH, CHAIRMAN, PRESIDENT, AND CEO OF CARLISLE COMPANIES (ARIZONA STATE UNIVERSITY, 2020)

Since this contract was a start-up project, not a lot of HR consequences were created yet. However, knowing I still needed to have my teams come in on time, instead of broadly stating I need them to send a time-off request, I told them I wanted them to request time off by Sunday of the previous week. I added a deadline of when I wanted the tasks to be done by, and by Monday the schedule was fairly fixed. If there are emergencies, I cannot do much about it, but they need to fulfill their end of the bargain.

I let them understand that in order for the project to continue, we must fulfill what the client wants. They expect us to have this amount of hours; without them, that cannot be achieved. By giving the team an exact day for when requests for time off need to be submitted, they have more clarity on what is expected of them. Of course, there are exemptions, but the point is if you can clarify expectations, clarify them so the team can do its job properly.

When we needed hours to be fully and accurately counted, my team had the best attendance. We had the closest schedule of projected hours worked versus actual hours worked, with 96 percent accuracy. In fact, when we had a competition around the most accurate hours, my team won.

What I tell the team is the three W's: the what, the why, and the when. The what is what are we discussing, which is scheduling, time off, and callouts. The why is why coming to work is important and how it affects the person next to you, behind you, or in front of you. The when is, when am I expecting time-off requests and when I will not be approving time-off requests. I told my team members to give me the hours they can work for. If they wanted to ask for a leave, they should submit a time-off request. My team was responsible and did what was asked of them, so I never had any issues with scheduling. And I also believe that people come to work on time and do not avoid it because the working environment is not something they want to run away from. We all know that feeling of not wanting to come to work because you do not like your workplace.

I have never said no to anyone's request for time off, mainly because if an individual does not work, they cannot work, and that is it. Yet, the team is still able to meet expectations. In influencing their inner motivation, most individuals will do what you need them to do.

BE THE PAINTER

The leader sometimes needs to be a painter. According to Melissa Lamson, CEO of Lamson Consulting in Phoenix, said leaders "need to paint the big picture for team members and bring the importance of their roles to the forefront. Team members need to know what their roles are, and why they matter" (Hirsch, 2019). Understanding the reason behind the actions leads people to connect more with the task. Leaders should clarify the goal as well as give information why they are taking such actions. You will be surprised that by doing so people will engage more with the project.

A part of clarity is also transparency. Be upfront with your team about expectations and why you have them. People want to do their job well; it is up to you to lead them or show them the best way to perform. You can start a task with a kickoff meeting to "jump-start interpersonal relationships and unite the team around a common purpose and goal," DeRosa said (Hirsch, 2019). The initial meeting can serve as a goal-setting introduction and a way to have the team collaborate with each other.

It serves everyone better to focus and execute on the task at hand than do multiple things at once. Clarity allows you and your team to focus on the task that should be achieved to propel the team to move forward. Clarity of roles gives the team the ability to identify what is expected of them in the position they currently are in and how to perform above and beyond the current role. Clarity of boundaries allows everyone some breathing space and not push an overbearing workload in an unrealistic time frame. Clarity is the beginning of the team's journey to success.

KNOWLEDGE NUGGETS:
- **Identify → Focus → Execute.** Know what your goal is, strive for it, and pursue it.
- **Role Clarity.** Clarify the to-dos—the scope of the job.
- **Clarity of Boundaries.** Know when to delineate work time and nonwork time.

- **Clarity of Vision.** Let the team know what future you are striving for.
- **Be the Painter.** Paint for your team your visualized future and explain why.

CHAPTER 7
GRAVITY OF FORTITUDE

Mike stands near the yellow line that marks the safety zone between the train tracks and the waiting passengers.

Another man walks behind him and stretches his arms forward and pushes Mike off the platform. Mike lands on the train tracks, and when he looks up, a light from an oncoming train stuns him, pinning him on the spot where he landed.

His friend, Chris, who was standing next to him, runs and jumps down the track. He lands on the train tracks with a thud, grabbing Mike's arm and bringing Mike up back to the passenger platform, just in the nick of time before the train passes by.

This is what majority of individuals would think what courage is: a physical form of bravery. If the word "courage" is uttered, a heroic image will pop up. However, courage is more than that.

If you read leadership books, you will often find courage as one of its topics, mainly because in a position of leadership where people seek your guidance, it takes courage to push through and decide where you will lead them. Courage is a timeless quality of a great leader.

I learned that courage was not the absence of fear, but the triumph over it. The brave man is not he who does not feel afraid, but he who conquers that fear.

NELSON MANDELA, ANTI-APARTHEID REVOLUTIONARY, STATESMAN, AND PHILANTHROPIST

What is courage? Courage, according to the Oxford Dictionary, "is the ability to do what frightens one" (Oxford Lexico, 2021). Courage does not mean there is an absence of fear. If fear is absent, then fear such an individual; they are rash and may cause harm to those around them. Courage is neither an excess in fear—that would be cowardice. Like many virtues, courage is on a sliding scale. On one end, rashness exists when there is an absence of fear. On the other end, there is the cowardice when overwhelming fear exists.

The courageous man withstands and fears those things which it is necessary [to fear and withstand] and on account of the right reason, and how and when it is necessary [to fear or withstand] them, and likewise in the case of being bold.

ANCIENT GREEK PHILOSOPHER, 2015

As a leader, you need to know what to do and when to do it. Rashness may cause further injuries. There is an aspect of courage that requires one to take educated risks. The movie *Kingdom of Heaven* rightfully depicts this courageous act of a leader knowing when to fight and knowing when to back down. The saying "you might have won the battle but you have not won the war" is something to take into consideration.

Where do you find yourself in the courage meter?

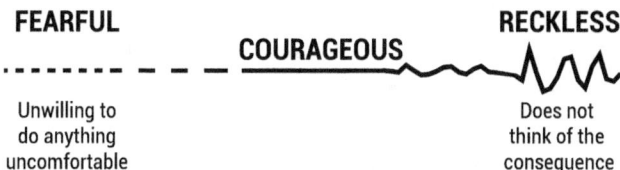

You do not want to land on either of the two extremes; you want moderation. If you are on the reckless side to the point where you are becoming too rash, it is dangerous. When you are unwilling to do anything, then your fear of fear itself will be your downfall. Courage, similar to other virtues, must be enhanced step by step.

Courage is one of the classic virtues any leader recognizes they need. It is part of the core values a leader must develop. In this dynamic world, there are times when ethical and moral standards are shaken and questioned. As a leader, you must have the courage to persist through the changes and stand your ground. You should not be hardheaded to get things your own way, but you should know when to take a stand for what you believe in. When the going gets tough, your team members must have your support.

Courage shows itself in many forms. Being a part of an organization means that you have to play by set rules. As a leader, if you think the rules set in place can be improved or need changing, you need the courage to change the status quo.

There will be times when you need to take the educated risk for the benefit of your team. When I was still an agent and not in a leadership position, I thought the information network was poorly structured, such as how documents and information were shared. When I became part of the leadership team, one member on my team commented, "It is hard to find the documents. They are everywhere." Being their leader, I had to act and fix the problem.

> *Courageous leaders take risks that go against the grain of their organizations. They make decisions with the potential for revolutionary change in their markets. Their boldness inspires their teams, energizes customers, and positions their companies as leaders in societal change.*
>
> BILL GEORGE, CEO OF MEDTRONIC (GEORGE, 2017)

That night I was sitting in the living room thinking of how to organize the documentation system in Slack. Then an idea sprouted. To make this idea possible, I needed to create a channel. Not knowing if we were allowed to create channels, I seized the initiative to create one, calling it our directory, where all the documents and links of the documents were arranged.

It became the informational network for my team to use, one in which I could easily add in all the information, and it was accessible to the team members. This required courage since I had to step out of my comfort zone and think outside the box to implement a solution I could use with my team. Additionally, I think this situation required courage because I implemented something new, meaning I am a pioneer.

Man cannot discover new oceans unless he has the courage to lose sight of the shore.

PHILIP DORMER STANHOPE, FOURTH EARL
OF CHESTERFIELD, BRITISH STATESMAN,
AND DIPLOMAT (GREENBERG, 2012)

Changemakers give themselves permission first. Beth Comstock, author of *Imagine It Forward,* director at Nike, and trustee of The National Geographic Society, saw that "time and again, especially with early managers at GE [where she] often worked with start-up founders. [She found they were] often looking for someone to give [them] permission." Beth pointed out that early managers or start-up founders seek for someone to give them the green light to go ahead and do things (Comstock, 2021).

She said, "A lot of change making is grabbing agency. It is about saying to yourself, 'I am just taking one small step.' It's behavior modification." Leaders are no strangers to change, and it requires courage to make that, to "take a small risk and the next time take a little bit bigger, it could be that first step. Give yourself a chance, grab agency, be *permission granting*" (Comstock, 2021). The funny thing about taking the lead is that when you look around the room you will realize that you are now the adult in the room. People look up to you and wait for your go, so when taking the lead, give yourself permission to be the adult. You can now determine when the green light starts.

Nonconformity, going against the grain, may be seen negatively and positively. As mentioned before, an educated risk is needed in the personal example I gave. I had taken the chance to implement something new within my team. First, it benefitted my team for me to do it. Second, it did not harm the organization, which is why I dared to take flight and had the faith to create something new.

As a virtual leader, this is particularly helpful. Although the virtual work environment started long ago, there is still confusion about governing it properly. With the increased pace of technological changes, one can encounter a situation in which the virtual organization is inefficient. As a virtual leader, you need the courage to implement some out-of-the-box solutions you discover or create.

So how does one build courage? I read an article that talks about how one man built up his courage by doing something uncomfortable each day. At first, he was overwhelmed by his emotions and was about to quit, but then he decided to continue his plan. If he were not to continue it, he would forever be unable to get it started. This guy would lie down with his back on the floor in the middle of the train and in other places where he went. Eventually, he noticed that the more he did that, the less he felt scared. This story shows that courage needs to be practiced daily. The more you exercise your courage, the braver you become and the more welcoming you are to newer experiences.

When I was in elementary school, I participated in school pageants. Being on stage then did not wholly eradicate my stage fright, but oddly enough, it made me more welcoming to different experiences.

Courage is a deliberate act; it requires deliberate practice. You can think of courage like a muscle. The more you exercise it, the stronger it gets. Here are the four ways you need to do to practice courage:

1. **Be permission granting.** Give yourself the green light to go ahead and pursue your dreams. I named my team "the sculptor," meaning the one who molds their own destiny. The sculptor is a proactive individual, not reactive. Be proactive.
2. **Be bold.** Do something that you are uncomfortable with. If you are afraid to present, present first in front of a friend or family and then reach out to larger groups. Be audacious.
3. **Be action oriented.** We often get so stuck in the analysis paralysis phase that the idea does not get executed. Execute your ideas. If they fail, then you have gained some lessons and experience. At least you tried.
4. **Have grit.** When it seems like there is an uphill battle and your decisions are challenged, this is the time when you need the courage to stand firm with your convictions. Hang in there, endure, stick to it, and persevere.

More often than not, the hard questions fall into the leader's lap. Sometimes, leaders fall into the situation of moral dilemmas, which causes distress for the individual. The distress is often caused by cognitive dissonance between what the organization wants and what the individual perceives as moral. Moral courage needs to be developed in a leader.

> *Acute manifestations of moral distress, if not acted upon and resolved, lead to moral residue, or the additional development over time of regret, anger, and*

> *frustration. [In the long term, the] cost of sustained moral distress can be absenteeism, morale issues, and poor productivity for the organization along with emotional exhaustion.*
>
> — COLE EDMONSON, MS, RN, FACHE, NEA-BC (EDMONSON, 2010)

Moral distress is rampant in any customer service occupation.

The American Association of Critical-Care Nurses has identified the 4 A's that helps nurses overcome moral distress (American Association of Critical-Care Nurses, 2021):

1. Affirm: Validate your feelings of distress.
2. Assess: Identify what is causing the distress.
3. Ask: Ask and figure out if you are feeling distressed. Part of figuring out how to fix the problem is knowing there is a problem.
4. Take Action: This one needs the most moral courage.
5. Repeat.

Courage is a general term. If we diced and scrutinized it, we would find there are several types.

THREE TYPES OF COURAGE:

According to Daniel Putman, PhD in Social Ethics, professor of philosophy, and author, courage can be divided into three: physical courage, psychological courage, and moral courage (Putman, 1997). Physical courage often exists when a man goes to war. Being in a virtual environment, physical courage is not as needed, so we will focus the on psychological courage and moral courage that a virtual leader encounters.

PSYCHOLOGICAL COURAGE

Vulnerability is often considered a weakness and something to avoid, yet my belief and experience is to the contrary.

LOUISE YOUNIE, GENERAL PRACTITIONER,
AND CLINICAL SENIOR LECTURER

Psychological courage, for example, can come about from watching a horror movie, looking at a picture of a snake, or getting an injection. Psychological courage "involves facing our deep-seated fear of psychological instability." It is the strength that allows an individual to overcome, confront, and work through the problems at hand (Putman, 1997).

Courage to tell others your shortcomings—I know, that is quite opposite of what you think courage would be, yet telling others where you fall short requires maturity and courage. Maturity acknowledges you are not perfect and do not know everything. Courage recognizes it is hard to show others your own vulnerability, especially among those who rely on you.

The biggest barrier to daring leadership is the armor we carry around—the thoughts, attitudes, behaviors, mannerisms and feelings—that make it almost impossible for us to show our real selves and express our true feelings.

COMMUNIQUE, 2021

Telling others your shortcomings shows them you are a work in progress. I often tell my team, "We are growing together. Push yourselves to be a better version of who you are now." When I first started my team, it was the first official leadership role I had. I explained this to them and asked them to bear with me. If we all help each other, we will grow together.

Brené Brown, a researcher and storyteller, said, "Allowing ourselves to be seen and known, that is, making ourselves vulnerable, allows us to connect in meaningful ways with others" (Younie, 2016). To share that you are vulnerable does not mean you are weak; it means you are strong enough to seek help when needed. Hardships are consistent in the human condition; we humans all share them. In a good setting, they will allow people to grow closer to each other.

In the end, my team grew out to be a very collaborative team, helping each other out and relying on one other. I did my due diligence by serving as their role model as well by being available to them when necessary and pushing them from the background to challenge themselves.

Vulnerability
Showing vulnerability makes one more human, easier to connect with. It is hard to connect in a virtual environment, so taking down a layer of the facade may very well be a key that allows you to connect with others. The process of being vulnerable requires courage—a lot of it. Kathy Ball-Toncic, a corporate and leadership coach and founder of The 262 Group, mentioned that a critical step in being a courageous leader and transform behaviors is tapping into people's vulnerabilities and fears. Knowing people's vulnerabilities and fears allows one to compliment those characteristics to the benefit of the individual and the team (Turunen, 2021).

Learn to destigmatize weaknesses and failures. Create an environment that allows an individual to comfortably seek help. If the individual feels unsafe or thinks they will be penalized for presenting their opinions or for making mistakes, people will often cocoon themselves for protection. Psychological courage will not be practiced. Instead, fear will overrule them in this scenario. Sometimes in a new environment, people should be encouraged to fail, to fail faster so they can figure out what works best. Make your team a safe space.

MORAL COURAGE

And most important, have the courage to follow your heart and intuition. They somehow already know what you truly want to become. Everything else is secondary.

STEVE JOBS, CO-FOUNDER, CHAIRMAN, AND CEO OF APPLE (GREENBERG, 2012)

Daniel Putman defines moral courage as the fear that revolves around the loss of ethical integrity or authenticity. A leader is often left with the hardest questions to answer, and this requires courage for the leader to take action amidst the overwhelming pressure surrounding the event (Putman, 1997).

From caring comes courage.

LAO TZU, CHINESE PHILOSOPHER AND WRITER (GREENBERG, 2012)

John is an entry level manager. He used to work as a lead technician over at IntelliSoft, a Samsung repair shop. He worked menial jobs to get by until he found his job through the Texas Workforce Commission. He started out as an agent and worked his way up to a management position.

John is one of my co-workers, dubbed as "Batman" at work by the agents, and rightfully so, with John's eagerness to help out the agents as best he can.

There was a time at work when we were asked to reduce hours. All teams needed to cut ten hours each day and a total of fifty per week. John didn't even ask any of his teammates to shave off hours. He explained that when leadership asked who was taking fewer hours, he reminded them that his team had just lost two people, so that was sixteen hours per day. He actually told leadership they owed his team hours since they were over the required amount.

After this conversation between John and leadership, John's suggestion was implemented for his team. Sometime later it was announced to all the supervisors they could not count the hours for the members who resigned.

John commented, "I wish everyone got away with that. You know, I felt bad [for other teams] but at the same time, you know, it was good. It's good for my teammates. They need those hours just as much as anybody else, you know, and so I try to protect them and stick up for them."

This act of courage by John allowed him to preserve the remaining hours for his team members. Amid the overwhelming pressure to reduce hours, John stood up for his team members and refused to give in.

I think the lower you are in the rung of leadership, the more necessary it is for you to practice moral courage. More often than not, a lot of your actions will be decided by the people above you. There will be times when you have to defend your team against decisions that are made by upper management.

Being terrified but going ahead and doing what must be done— that's courage. The one who feels no fear is a fool, and the one who lets fear rule him is a coward.

PIERS ANTHONY, ENGLISH AMERICAN
AUTHOR (GREENBERG, 2012)

Have your team know that you have their backs. In the new virtual environment, the sudden shift in workspace and habits has some people scared. It requires the leader to dive in first and have the courage to pursue the unknown to lead the team. Lead courageously in what is now called "the new normal."

Courage, at the end of the day, will help you stand your ground and fight through adversity. In this fast-paced working environment and the inevitable changes we will all go through, your courage will be the torch that will allow you to hold your light, for you to embrace the new environment and alleviate the anxiety that your team has.

I tell my team that, as long as we are all in this together, we will be just fine and better than the day before. If you have courage to lead the trek through an unknown path, your team will surely follow. Those who make the journey worthwhile will surely be rewarded. Like the Latin proverb *Publius Vergilius Maro* (Virgil) said, "*Audentes Fortuna Iuvat*," which can be translated as "Fortune favors the bold."

Courage is rightly esteemed the first of human qualities... because it is quality which guarantees all others.

WINSTON CHURCHILL, FORMER PRIME MINISTER, WRITER, AND ORATOR

Moral courage requires self-certainty. Though you may not have the answer, you are still required to ground yourself. Show you are in control of the uncertain situation so your team can feel at ease and will be able to perform their job better. The leader sets the tone.

Courage requires physical toughness, moral toughness, and psychological toughness. In the virtual workspace, psychological and moral courage are prominently challenged. Courage to lead requires one to give oneself the permission to take action, to show the vulnerabilities and know that it does not define one but instead allows one to identify one's strengths.

KNOWLEDGE NUGGETS:
- **Psychological Courage.** Courage that allows you to overcome your fears.
- **Moral Courage.** Leans toward ethics and good versus evil. Have the courage to stand for what you believe in.

CHAPTER 8

PROFESSIONAL IDEATION

Part of what differentiates a leader from the flock is that the leader initiates, unifies, and solves. Problem-solving capabilities of an individual are part of the reason why they are placed in a position to lead. While others discuss what may go wrong and whatnot, the leader is already taking action toward the solution of the issue.

Once you are in a leadership position, people look to you for answers. You need both a strategic and creative mind to be able to cruise through problems.

The virtual environment poses new sorts of problems, such as computer issues, company issues, and people issues. To resolve these issues, you have to build structures, the skeleton to help your team do its job.

When you think of a business, you may think there is lack of creativity, but creativity really is the *source of growth* and the force that propels an organization to change for the better.

People think structuring your workplace hinders creativity. I think it allows for more creative thinking. The more optimized and organized your workplace is, the more space there is for creative thinking or what I call strategic planning.

I often use this to my advantage. Once I get rid of the time-consuming tasks I need to do, I get to do more of the things I like, innovating different ways to progress the team and the organization's goals. I personally love strategizing on ways I can influence the team members to perform on their own as independent individuals and achieve the vision of the organization. I tend to manipulate the environment the team is in so it will help them perform tasks in a certain way.

When the pandemic hit, more and more teams went virtual—even the teams that never had been in a virtual environment before. Creativity in a virtual environment needs the individual to experiment with different mediums. How do you best conduct your team meetings in Microsoft Teams, Zoom, or Webex? Inside Microsoft Teams and Zoom, there is an option to use a whiteboard. You can use it to play games with your team or do some group activity, which can help you foster the team culture.

For leaders who are building their virtual environment from scratch, being strategic and creative at what we do will help with creating structures. Structures are important if you want to create a successful virtual team. It allows for the fluidity of movement when you are systematic and optimized.

Part of what makes a leader successful is their ability to be agile when changes are presented. Being agile is a quality of a strategic/creative individual.

SHARP AND FOCUSED MEETINGS
Creativity is there to enhance. Vinay Raman, CEO of CAARMO, mentioned that the EOS system is helpful. The EOS, or Entrepreneurial Operating System, is the system he uses in his project. EOS was created by Gino Wickman, an author and entrepreneur. EOS is an operating system that focuses on six key components: People, Data, Vision, Issues, Process, and Traction.

Having the same meeting time every day creates consistency. People crave consistency, especially amid the pandemic. People's lives feel out of control and individuals will cling to the opportunity of any form of control. It became one thing people did not have to worry about when meetings, tasks, and expectations became consistent.

When I was talking to Jennifer Davis, chief marketing officer, author of *Well Made Decisions*, and former product marketing lead for Amazon Web Services, she told me about this creative idea that came about when she found an excerpt from the book *Conscious Leadership* by John Mackey, CEO of Whole Foods:

> At Whole Foods Market, before we end any meeting, we ask a question: Would anyone like to appreciate a fellow team member? Whether it's a store team meeting or a strategy session with the executive leadership team, we never leave without opening the floor for people to honor one another's positive contributions. It's one of the ways we strive as a company to operationalize a virtue that's too often overlooked in business: **love.**
>
> JOHN MACKEY, CEO OF WHOLE FOODS
(FACT OF THE DAY 1, 2020)

Using this excerpt and her knowledge about EOS, she added another section of her meeting—leaving a "positive note." To give you a quick background, the EOS meeting has this structure: (Wickman and Bouwer, 2017).

1. Segue: Team conversation/engagement
2. Scorecard: Scoring data getting discussed
3. Rocks: Discussing issues that are preventing your company from flourishing that need to be fixed and addressed
4. Client/employee headlines
5. To-dos: Discussing shared and individual tasks
6. Issues list: Any issues that needs to be resolved
7. Conclusion: Summary of the meeting

In the conclusion, when topics are summarized, Jennifer included a positive note, which includes staff appreciation amongst her team members and other teams. Jennifer "took the appreciations outside of [her] team and sent personal notes to those mentioned, copying in their manager and the person who had mentioned them, with specific feedback on why they and their work were appreciated." The positive note created a good karma cycle in Jennifer's team and in other departments that were working with them.

Depending on what type of work your team does, the structure and length of the meeting will differ. For my team, there is no need to hold lengthy meetings. The stand-ups serve as a pulse check for the team and mainly revolve around daily updates. Our daily fifteen-minute work-focused stand-up with the team has this structure.

1. Segue: You can do a question of the day here during this time. Allow people in your team ample time to talk. These short questions allow your team members to have watercooler conversations, which are a great way to build team rapport.
2. Daily updates: Any updates involving the company and the tasks will be addressed during this time.
3. Questions: Any questions can be asked here, from work questions to getting to know your team member questions.
4. Positive messages: This is a spontaneous ask to encourage a motivational mindset. When you allow spontaneity in the day, it provides a more authentic view of the individuals in the team and their current state of mind.

For days when we do not have a lot of updates or questions, I allow the team to talk to each other. I turn my microphone on mute, indicating they have free rein during this time. More questions do arise and I answer them, but sometimes the team just talks about random things. I give them this time because of the few touch points we have in a virtual/remote work. This becomes another opportunity for them to meet and talk with other team members. I make it intentional to introduce this as a touch point.

Daily tasks that may be harder and involve more people may need to be reviewed, or a process may need to be created. If it's something that is done daily but is easy enough, allow more creativity for this area.

MAKE SURE THE SHOE FITS: BEHAVIORAL STRUCTURE
I work at a start-up company, and the account we are in is the major project the company has. Since it's a new project, not a lot of structure has been introduced yet, so the project itself is similar to any team just starting out moving to a virtual environment.

With a creative mind one can come up with several strategies; one can influence the way a team performance goes. I utilize multiple structural strategies when I lead. However, the primary structure I rely on is the *behavioral structure* of my team. Is my team dependent or independent? You can gauge team performance on behavior simply by observing if your team needs your input for every single decision. Is the team cooperative and willing to work with one another?

The next generation of workers will be Generation Z. Part of the behavioral strategy you can use in leading this generation is through purpose.

While purpose has long been linked to retention and engagement, I would argue that when it comes to Gen Z, it's actually a critical component of getting new talent in the door.

DANIEL GOLEMAN, PSYCHOLOGIST, AUTHOR, AND SCIENCE JOURNALIST (GOLEMAN, 2021)

PRIORITIZE
1. Part of strategy is choosing your battles. I found some people just do more and more tasks to keep themselves busy—not productive, but BUSY.
    a. There is a document review board on our team that creates a lot of documents, and some get thrown out. Going into a meeting, I found out they sometimes redress some information that was already presented. Sometimes, these documents become additional clutter and cause overcommunication.
    b. Choose your battles.
    c. Clarify. This is used to address the issue of busy versus productive. The first step with clarity is identifying the issue and figuring out how to best resolve this issue efficiently.
2. Less is more and more is less.
    d. From my interviews, a lot of virtual teams have a hard time establishing the foundations and/or protocols that will help them navigate the virtual space.

HOW TO IMPROVE VIRTUAL WORK ENVIRONMENTS

Here's what I learned from my interviews on how to improve the virtual work environment.
1. Protocols need to be detailed. Explain how to navigate the steps of the protocol and show images along with protocols. Some people have difficulty navigating the virtual environment, especially when the company uses multiple applications or systems, which can confuse workers. Protocols are critical in establishing an efficient team and a successful workplace.
2. Be creative. Factors that contribute to strategies are the out-of-the-box thinking. Creativity in a virtual space

increases through the use of tools and the way people engage.
3. Begin with the end in mind.

"Forty-four percent of remote workers reported a lack of the right infrastructure, platforms, and data that they need to be fully productive at work" (Wrike, 2021). For some teams, they struggle partly because they have not established a structure since the virtual environment is new to them or there is lack of knowledge on which tools to use, and for others it is the lack of understanding of the virtual environment itself.

Fifty-two percent of remote employees mentioned that they lack the requisite training to efficiently use work management platforms where they are available.

WRIKE, 2021

To create a productive team, one strategy that you can do is to strengthen your structure around how to do things. Jaime Jay is the owner of Bottleneck Distant Assistants who has outsourced distant assistants from the Philippines for fifteen years and leads a team of fifty members and is the author of the book *Quit Repeating Yourself*. Jaime and his team are 100 percent remote and have never met in person. One of the challenges that Jaime and his team experiences is ensuring that systems, processes, and workflows are in order "literally step by step."

Jaime shared an example when he was in an office environment in corporate America. For twelve years he was working in the corporate world. Jaime noticed that being remote forces you to document, step by step, every single protocol.

Jaime saw that by having the documentation ready, people would have a reference on what to do and how to do it and which portion you needed to click on your screen to get to the desired result. Documentation also allows more room for scalability, and team members will be more "confident [when] they can execute all the tasks given them, because it's done in the same way that's already been approved."

Documentation with images can help especially when onboarding multiple people in your team. If you onboard people virtually, everything becomes more complicated. In a collocated workspace, a tap on the shoulder may only be needed to get help from another member and a few minutes for them to point out which direction you go on the screen. In a remote workspace, a few minutes of work may turn into an hour as your team member tries to tell you where to go and you have difficulty navigating the screen.

When starting out your remote team, you will have difficulty recognizing which aspects of your team and tasks need to be structured and how to do so. However, you will eventually appreciate the need for a structure for a more effective and progressive team.

Jaime: "It took me a while to realize that I was doing things over and over and it was such a waste of time. Why don't I document this? So it took a while for me to understand how important systems processes and workflows were. All these companies out there [have] developed systems that's why franchising is so popular because somebody doesn't want to create all those systems, they want to go and buy a business with all the systems already there."

In a new virtual space where your team has not established the infrastructure that you want to operate in, innovation and creativity is greatly needed. Creativity in this case is more about strategic thinking, which allows everyone in the team to establish a work setting that can get you up and running.

Good is a leader who can creatively flourish and great is the leader who inspires creativity in others.

USE CONCEPT BOARDS

Concept boards can be used whether you are working virtually or not. In the case of a virtual environment, the medium may change from an actual board to a software. In this case, you can be creative in what you want to use. Concept boards are a great way to sort out ideas with your team when planning for a project. One of my managers used MURAL, a digital workspace for visual collaboration, to get feedback from the team.

When our team had to transition and split up to different teams, our supervisor created a MURAL diagram. Within this diagram, he had a hexagon that was divided into six triangles. Each triangle contained the name of everyone on the team. He then said to grab the notepad available on MURAL and add in anything we knew about each team member. So each of us got a notepad and created a short description about the team member. We then used those notes to thank each person for being a great teammate. It was a great group exercise that fostered and left good impressions of each individual in the team and their contributions.

I thought it was a creative team building exercise, so I implemented it on my team. I did not have access to MURAL and did not want to pay out of pocket for it since I would not be using it that frequently. Consequently, I got creative. I created a team channel in Slack and named it "the-sculptor-spotlight." I told the team we would be using this to do shout-outs.

I had everyone come to the meeting and type in their names and post them in the channel. I then told the team that, for each individual name that is posted, click reply and add in any positive information that you know about this team member. On the notes, they wrote how team members helped them and how generous they were.

This strategy has a few purposes. I used this activity to foster team motivation and teamwork, and it also provided me notes that I added in the journal for each team member. I basically had access to information of how well the team members were doing and what contributions they gave, allowing me to present each individual in a better light to human resources and their team members. This activity made the team members happy hearing all the good things about them, and they also came to appreciate each other.

For the HR perspective, I gave them information about the team member, not something coming from me but from other agents. This gave much more genuine feedback about who each individual was in the team. I took a picture of it and shared it everywhere. I mainly shared it when I advocated for the team member to be considered for a project. Sometimes it's not necessarily the technology but more so the strategy that you use. Be creative! Flex those brains.

AN ALERT ON ALERTS

Be clear in your communication and be strategic on how you communicate.

This is where we have to be cautious about communication. Technology has made it so easy for us to create alerts that, in just a few minutes, you can automate a lot of reminders. For example, one of the supervisors made it possible to automatically email everyone assigned to receive an alert whenever a post or reply on a certain channel was created. It is a brilliant idea; he makes a post in a channel where vital tasks need6 to be done. Suddenly you receive it in your email, and you know what needs your attention. Technology has made it easy to create alerts and reminders.

First of all, everyone was on Slack and was in the channel. Assuming that someone may not see, he created the alert. That is where the hidden devil hid: it just so happened that every—I mean every—reply got sent to your email. There were around twenty-two level one supervisors. For each task published, a good amount of supervisors would reply "done" to indicate the task was finished. When that happened, suddenly you would get ten messages in your email just saying "done."

The devil was the noise. This created an average of ten emails per task—a bit much, so they changed the process. Level two supervisors decided to have us reply using emojis to indicate we had done a task. If we had further questions, we just created a new thread in another Slack channel to continue the conversation there, so as not to trigger the alert.

My second example of overcommunication still revolves around alerts. It is easy to get lost in team communication channels. The greater the amount of people, the greater the communication traffic it creates. Mentions such as "@here" and "@channel" in Slack trigger this alert where it displays this red circle next to the channel to indicate that someone wanted to inform you of a certain post, and they used "@here" to alert everyone online or "@channel" to alert everyone with access to that channel.

Now, there is a point when these alerts are so overused that people will become tone-deaf to them; it desensitizes people. For example, for "@here's" for other groups that talk about updates on their teams, I end up closing my eyes on those. With the amount of "@here's" you get, you end up dropping the ball on some of them especially if the message is not an important one.

Creativity is a thinking-out-of-the-box type of action, while strategy allows for a more structured approach to things. As you trudge around the virtual environment, see the issues you are having as an opportunity to make each process more fluid. Creativity paired with strategy is a heart-and-soul mixture that allows one the opportunity to build something that is repeatable, efficient, and effective.

KNOWLEDGE NUGGETS:
- **Sharp and Focused Meetings.** Structure your meetings so you can get the most of it and not just scheduling a meeting for the sake of having a meeting scheduled. Do not get stuck in the meeting frenzy. Follow the agenda.

- **Make Sure the Shoe Fits: Behavioral Structure.** Adjust the way you lead depending on the team member. Compliment their behavior to bring out the best of their talents.
- **Prioritize.** Know what to work on rather than winging it or spending time on things that don't matter. Focus.
- **How to Improve Virtual Work Environments.** Think big while adding structure so people can use whatever you created.
- **Use Concept Boards.** Write it out so it is easy to follow what you want to happen, so you and your team can always go back to it.
- **An Alert on Alerts.** Be strategic on what you want to emphasize. If you emphasize everything, people may become tone-deaf to what you really are aiming for. Decrease unnecessary noise.

PART II

VIRTUAL WORLD ENHANCEMENT

CHAPTER 9

TO SPEAK OR NOT TO SPEAK

—

Did you hear that?

That is the sound of silence.

One of the overlooked parts of communication is *silence*.

Use *QUIET* as a communication strategy.

Silence can be used as a communication strategy. Keep silent and allow your team members to speak. Two, use silence to not overflow your team communication channel with a lot of information. Sometimes in communication, less is more and more is less—simplify things. Sometimes, the team needs to ruminate and bake the bread in the oven before they can give you the finished product.

Communication helps us establish a connection with others. Without communication, we could not build a team, nor would we be able to work together. As mentioned previously, trust requires communication. Communication builds rapport. Bill Gates once said that any tool that enhances communication will affect how well people can connect and learn from each other (Meier, 2021). Tools are there to enhance and help us; they serve as a medium for us to fully communicate our whole self.

Communication in a virtual setting poses a few advantages and disadvantages. One of the advantages is that you can easily call and send a message to your team member; the opposite of this would be overcommunication and communication misinterpretation. Other communication issues are ghosting and work-life balance.

An article written by Deloitte Denmark on leading virtual teams said that over "70 percent of business professionals expect the use of online collaboration platforms to increase in the future" (Deloitte, 2021). To effectively communicate, the team must decide what mode or communication tool they are going to use.

ASYNCHRONOUS VS. SYNCHRONOUS COMMUNICATION
Technology is a helper, tool, and medium.

Claire Hastwell, Content Marketing Manager and co-author of *Women in the Workplace,* said that "if your company doesn't currently use an internal messaging system, now is an ideal time to start" (Hastwell, 2021). With the already booming shuffle toward virtual work, it is now clearer than ever that communication happens using a different technology than when we chat face-to-face.

In a virtual setting, the right tool will enhance your ability to communicate with your team clearly and concisely. "The quality of a team leader's communication is a critical determinant of team success" (Newman, Ford, and Marshall, 2019).

The tools can be divided into synchronous and asynchronous. Synchronous tools are helpful when the team needs immediate access to conversations within the team. This is especially helpful when complex problems need immediate resolutions.

There are many tools such as Discord and Slack, which are similar to instant messaging apps. SharePoint is a way to share live documents. Zoom and Webex are video call platforms. Asynchronous communication would include emails, project management tools, direct mails, text messages—those that do not necessitate an immediate reply.

The responsibility of the leader is to ensure each team member has the resources they need. Virtual communication may impose a problem in that some announcements may get overlooked.

MATCHING COMMUNICATION TOOL WITH TEAM CULTURE/ENVIRONMENT

I met Kelly Barrett, an associate consultant, around fall 2020. She became my mentor for Girls Who Consult. She mentioned that when she and her team "first started working remote, it was really difficult because [they] didn't really have the tools that [they] needed."

Her team used Slack in the beginning and then transitioned to using Teams, because with Microsoft Teams "you can also do internal and external calls so people don't have to be a part of your group in Teams to be able to call them." The capability of Teams was useful for work, especially for those who need to do external calls. It made it efficient for their group when using Teams. When they have client calls, they send out a link for the client to join the team call. Different software has similar functionalities, but one may best fit your team's needs.

There is a difference in how Slack and Teams work. With Slack, you can communicate with anyone in your workspace, meaning they have to be on your Slack. Kelly preferred Microsoft Teams because it allowed her to do external and internal calls to connect with her team and clients. For virtual teams, she discovered you need to "communicate fifteen times more than you'd expect." More communication is needed when you are working in a physically distant workspace.

It is great to identify another tool for communication in case of emergencies. For example, at my work, one day around noon, Slack began to be glitchy. Having no other communication tools with my team, we all had to settle for emails. Emails are hard to use when you want immediate replies.

Twenty people emailing me their information and asking me questions was an information overload. In one hour, I had approximately thirty emails. For our job, which requires constant communication, sending emails was a pain. Luckily, I remembered my mentor Kelly had mentioned Microsoft Teams. I quickly created a group chat for my teams.

Reinforcing Claire Hastwell's point that messaging systems enable quick and efficient communication among team members without straining their inboxes, my team quickly got ahold of using Teams and was able to work through the glitchy Slack issues.

Kelly also figured messaging was confusing and it was better for her to just get on a phone call with her team members, because by the time she deciphered the message and figured out what they were trying to ask and responded, it was going to take twice as long as a call.

Figuring out which tool is helpful for you and your team is a necessity. Kelly mentioned that in the beginning, they had people use different types of communication tools and "getting ready for [the] client calling, be [it] Skype, Zoom, like, which one is it? And you'd have to go to all of them and [she] think sometimes [they] use uber conference so [she] thinks having everything in one place really helped [them] a lot." Streamlining communication reduces frustration for individuals on both ends.

Figuring out the best communication tool for your team is a must-do.

> *While technology standards are increasing all the time, technology often has a way of failing just when you need it most. Zoom allows you to dial into video calls from a landline, for those who can't use their computers for whatever reason. You may have other preferred backup methods.*
>
> BREE CAGGIATI, SEO SPECIALIST AND WRITER (CAGGIATI, 2021)

Know the primary tool you will be using. Bear in mind that technology does fail and be ready to do some troubleshooting or use a secondary option.

COMMUNICATION GAPS

"Ghosting" occurs when an individual does not reply to any of your messages. This can pose quite a threat, especially in a 100 percent remote workplace. In the safety of the remote location, one can easily say they did not read the email. One thing that can help you cure this ailment is to set clear expectations with your team members. Perhaps mention they are expected to answer if they are on the clock but are not expected to if it is outside work hours. This sets a boundary between members and fosters a space where work-life balance is respected.

Set expectations. It's hard to figure out what a person wants. The team members are not mind readers; be clear with them with what you want. Explain things as simply as when people are expected to reply to emails, DMs, or phone calls.

According to Michelle LaBrosse, founder and CEO of Cheetah Learning and author of *Cheetah Project Management* and *Cheetah Negotiations,* "When people are working remotely, it's important that you define what your rules of responsiveness are for your culture" (LaBrosse, 2010).

I tell my team I do not expect them to answer my direct messages during lunchtime and that they can answer me once they come back. I do not want them to keep looking at their messages while at lunch. It is their break, and I respect that. This also partly touches the topic of clarity with boundaries. Clarify to everyone what expectations are to reduce frustrations between both sides. Individuals who are aware what is asked of them are more likely to perform better compared to a counterpart who does not know the expectations.

It is hard to connect with team members when you work remotely. You can no longer drop by the office and talk about what is going on. Instead, you are left to schedule a meeting and by the time the meeting comes, you will no longer be interested in saying what you planned on saying.

According to a survey conducted by Culture Wizard in 2010, virtual teams differed most from face-to-face teams in three areas: managing conflict (73 percent), making decisions (69 percent), and expressing opinions (64 percent) (RW3 Culture Wizard, 2010).

COMMUNICATION METHODS

Creating virtual spaces and rituals for celebrations and socializing can strengthen relationships and lay the foundation for future collaboration.

DHAWAN AND CHAMORRO-PREMUZIC, 2018

As the leader of your group, you should set up events where your team members can gather. Other communication events that you can establish are doing daily huddles and a virtual open office. Daily huddles are where your operational discussions can take place, and you can start the meeting with some icebreakers.

Have everyone in your team answer the icebreaker questions. Icebreaker questions are simple questions that can be answered in one word or a few words, such as, "What's your favorite ice cream flavor?" This will allow the quiet members of the group some speaking time. After the icebreaker question, you may proceed with the operational meetings or updates.

Aside from the daily huddles, you can have an open office around one or two hours a day, where any of your team members can hop and talk to you or other members of the group. In Zoom, you can create breakout rooms for communications that require privacy while still giving others from the group a space to talk.

A team member sent me this message: "Thank you for your good leadership, direction and the open communication that you fostered in 'the-sculptor.'"

I host an open office as an optional social space where team members can hop onto Zoom for an hour at the end of the day and talk to each other. Make time for others to talk to each other, because team members appreciate an open social time. Sometimes team members stay even if they are off the clock and are not getting paid, since they enjoy the teams' company. I remember a team member who had time off who came to the open office meet to chat with the rest of the team.

Be creative in your communication method. Rachel Valdez, head of global talent management at PowerToFly, has TGIIF meetings (Thank God It's Inspiration Friday) where her team members share stories of what inspired them that week, as well as what they're looking forward to doing that weekend. "Since we are a remote team, these connection points make all the difference and we actually see an increase in productivity and general well-being on the team" (Grow, 2019).

The following ways are great for team building and a way to get your team members to talk and for you to listen. Build a culture of inclusivity and encourage discussion between team members.

Providing the team the time to get to know each other is beneficial in the long run. Dr. Dan Caprar, senior lecturer in international business at University of Sydney, recommends bringing the team together, enabling them to get to know each other. This allows for plenty of scope to work remotely later (Caggiati, 2019). Yes, this may cost the company money, but the investment is worthwhile because people easily reach the stage where they work effectively and efficiently together.

COMMUNICATION AS A RELATIONSHIP BRIDGE

In a virtual setting where communication is difficult to control, listening is a great way to balance the situation. Listening is a form of communication that allows the leader to identify where the team needs to improve. To be a great leader, you have to first be a great listener.

William Ury is a negotiator and an author who dreams of creating a world where people do less talking and more listening, which would revolutionize communication. One of his experiences in managing conflicts was with President of Venezuela Hugo Chavez. In this particular talk, the country of Venezuela was under intense conflict between the political opposition and the government, so extreme that people feared a civil war would break out (TEDx Talks, 2015).

President Chavez asks Ury what he thought about the issue, to which Ury replied, "I have been talking to the opposition and that there seems to [be] progress."

Chavez asked, "What do you mean progress?"

After thirty minutes of discussion, the president asked, "So, Ury, what should I do?"

He said the president should propose a truce so the people could enjoy the festivities, since last year they were unable to do so. The president's demeanor changed, and he agreed it was a great idea.

Ury had listened intently to the president, enabling him to make a resolution that delighted Chavez. By listening, he allowed the president to be heard, building a connection between them. This made the other person more open to his resolution; thus, it made it easier to influence the other person.

You do not connect with people where you are. You connect with people by finding out where they are. Leaders listen, learn, and they lead. Most of the cues are found when they listen.

JOHN MAXWELL, AMERICAN AUTHOR,
SPEAKER, AND PASTOR

The same goes for the people you are leading: the best way to influence them is to listen to them. To genuinely listen is to hear things through their lens, find out what they need, and help them.

Listening fosters understanding, and understanding helps with resolving issues, may it be personal or work related. As a leader, you can help resolve conflicts and allow the individuals to express their opinions.

Listening is how you read people. Listening may be the golden key that opens the door to human relationship.

WILLIAM URY, NEGOTIATOR AND
AUTHOR (TEDX TALKS, 2015)

Listening is a communication style that will help you build rapport with the people you are leading. Lead by listening, and those who follow you will listen as well.

We have two ears and one mouth so that we can listen twice as much as we speak.

EPICTETUS, GREEK STOIC PHILOSOPHER

All you need to do to be a better listener is to actively listen to the person you are conversing with. Do not think so much about your reply and place more concern in understanding what the person is telling you. When I was leading my team, I stumbled upon an article that said the person who talks the most in the meeting rates the meeting higher in productivity. Having that in mind, I focus on having the team members talk.

When I host my meetings, I start with the question of the day and segue into the updates. At the end, I offer my team the time to ask questions or talk to each other. Meetings are task oriented, which causes social isolation if people do not speak with each other. So I give the team the chance to speak with each other before they go back to their own tasks. By allowing them more time to talk, I am able to identify their concerns, and when they are reduced or resolved, that may greatly improve their mood.

LACK OF 360 VIEW

A couple of times my family members would pop in and open the door to my room while I was in a meeting. I would have to shoo them away without showing my hands on the camera. This proves my point that we never know the entirety of what goes on in the moment when people are not in the same location as us. Clarity is much needed, so there might be times when more clarifying questions need to be asked.

Ana Simpson, a remote manager, has extensive experience of leading people remotely. She was situated in Romania and had teams reporting to her from Greece and Bulgaria.

Ana Simpson mentioned, "The insight you see about the person when you are in a meeting is only the screen they are displayed on." You will never know what happens outside the boundaries of that screen. "I think more questions are being needed in the virtual environment, because sometimes you cannot catch everything from the body language because of the lack of body language or the face."

We do not know what different scenarios are going on in someone else's brain. So that's why it's important to ask as many questions as we can in order to make sure we are capturing the 360 understanding of the situation.

VIDEO CONFERENCING SOFTWARE
Take advantage of video conferencing softwares such as Zoom, Google Meet, and Webex.

I manage a team across all those Asian markets, so for us to stay in contact [we need to use video]
MICHAEL CHETNER, HEAD OF ASIA PACIFIC

AT ZOOM (CAGGIATI, 2021)

When people went virtual in the past, they had to use phones without any option to have a video call. Video calls are amazing—they give you another touch point with another individual.

Adrian Ward, CEO of KairoX Nation, mentioned during our interview that one of the advantages that differentiates a video call from a voice call is that you gain access to another set of information, such as facial expressions, shoulder shrugs, and so on.

Adrian said, "People are energy," and more energy is felt "because I can see you." Energy formation is felt in several ways:

- Voice: "I could feel your energy just by voice because voice is vibration and when you talk."
- Facial features and body gestures: "When you're smiling or your, your eyes are paying attention, and your body is happy."

Adrian continued, "It's cool—we don't have to be in front like in the same place to feel each other."

According to the article by FOND, a SaaS platform, "Off-topic Slack channels replace watercooler banter, and pre-meeting chatter happens over Zoom instead of during the walk to the boardroom. Modern problems demand modern solutions, and when it comes to building culture virtually, technology can be a manager's best" (FOND, 2021).

Use technology to your advantage.

COMMUNICATION ADD-ONS

New tools have made their way to connecting one other, coming closer to what it is in person. Dr. Riordan mentioned humans are continually exploring and creating ways to make distant communications more similar to an in-person communication environment. We have introduced emojis and GIFs to portray not only a smiling face but also show body gestures.

Dr. Monica Riordan, who has PhD in experimental psychology from the University of Memphis, introduced an emoji study. Her primary research area is exploring the way in which people are able to communicate emotions in computer-mediated environments.

In the absence of facial features in a virtual environment, emojis place a certain role in virtual messaging. Emojis clarify or disambiguate messages. In some instances, emojis add more clarification to the message than when more words were added (Riordan, 2017).

Emojis are often used to convey emotions that are harder to express with words and are complementary and not a substitute for text-based messages. Emojis help enhance and maintain social relationships. Emojis add character to what would have been a stale environment (Riordan, 2017). They are useful as a resource to comments that do not necessarily need a word response. For example, when we go to lunch, my team members let me know and I can reply using a food emoji and another emoji once they come back.

> *An e-mail message is accompanied by an emoticon, the effect of the message can change significantly for a reader. Specifically, when a positive message is accompanied by a positive emoticon, the message increases in positivity and happiness than the message without the emoticon—in other words, the valence is interpreted the same direction, but at a greater intensity when the emoticon is present. It seems, then, that emoticons are intended to convey affective information—not enough to alter the valence of the message itself, but enough to alter the intensity of the effect.*
>
> DR. MONICA RIORDAN, PROFESSOR OF EXPERIMENTAL PSYCHOLOGY

At first, I thought emojis were unprofessional and should not be used. However, I noticed engagement between conversations increased when I used emojis. It serves as an add-on to text messages. Sometimes, it can stand alone as a placeholder or a form of acknowledgment that you have read the message. When I post an update, some of my team members would add a thumbs-up to indicate "OK" or a check mark to indicate "complete" and that they have read the message.

> *One way to ensure effective cross-cultural communication is to create a mini-culture within your company. This won't necessarily match the home country of the organization or that of international workers, but will be a hybrid of sorts aimed at creating ideal working conditions for all involved.*
>
> BREE CAGGIATI, SEO SPECIALIST AND WRITER (CAGGIATI, 2019)

Use of emojis as a tool to use for culture building is discussed in the emotional intelligence chapter.

You have to keep in mind that an emoji will not replace real communication. So if the response needs more than an emoji, respond appropriately and do not fall in the emoji trap where you use emojis to replace your communication.

Agent: *sends me an update*

Me: *Uses thumbs up emoji to indicate that I saw*

Also me: Thank you for the update!

Two separate things are happening here. I used the emoji as an indication to say, "Okay, I saw your message," and I followed it up with a "thank you" to tell them what I wanted to say. Emojis and GIFs are a great addition to virtual communication.

At the end of the day, tools for communication are just tools. They are there to help and not disable. The human aspect of communication will always be the driver; you are the captain, so sail your ship to the right direction.

> *It's not necessarily about whether you use GIFs or emojis or all kinds of other things—we need to focus on clarity in our communication and disambiguating our message and on shaping a message to an audience.*
>
> DR. MONICA RIORDAN, PROFESSOR OF EXPERIMENTAL PSYCHOLOGY

Communication in a remote environment is one of the most talked-about topics. Leaders are finding different ways to communicate with their teams effectively. In a virtual work environment, communication now needs a tool to transport the thought from person to person. While in an office environment, that tool is not a necessity but a luxury, since we can always go talk to the individual face to face without the necessary equipment.

Aside from tools, clarity and intentionality are definitely must-haves, clarity in that your message should not be so brief that people will have to figure out your encrypted message, or too long that it causes confusion. Intentionality is needed when communicating. You no longer have random hallway meetings. Instead, you have to intentionally create space and time for your team to communicate. Building a relationship in a virtual environment requires high intentionality, so make time to waste time and build a relationship with others.

KNOWLEDGE NUGGETS:
- **Asynchronous vs. Synchronous Communication.** Know the difference between the communication types and let your team know about your expectations.
- **Matching Communication Tool with Team Culture/ Environment.** Figure out which tools best fit your workplace and know how your team communicates.
- **Communication Gaps.** Say NO to ghosting and let people know what and when you expect answers from them.
- **Communication Methods.** Introduce icebreakers and other ways to nudge your team members out of their shells and get them talking.
- **Communication as a Relationship Bridge.** Listen and understand.
- **Lack of 360 View.** Understand the disadvantages of not being able to see the entire room and use it to your advantage.
- **Video Conferencing Software.** Use video as another touch point.
- **Communication Add-Ons.** Use GIFs and emojis as conversation starters or something to complement your communication with others. They are both complementary aids, and you can define their functionality within your team.

CHAPTER 10

ENVIRONMENT CULTIVATION

What are the components that make the best virtual environment?

Simply put, anything that promotes psychological safety is the way you should describe what the best work environment is. It is easy enough to identify this. If your team can easily own up to its mistakes without the fear of being rebuked, you've cultivated a place where people feel safe. Part of feeling safe is having a community that has your back.

Gardner and Matviak wrote in the *Harvard Business Review*, "Leaders, especially those who are not used to managing virtual teams, may feel stressed about keeping the team on track. Under these circumstances it is tempting to become exclusively task-focused. To address these challenges, making time for personal interaction is more important than ever" (Gardner and Matviak, 2020).

An open and welcoming environment will serve your company well with an increase in worker satisfaction and loyalty. People often forgo a better salary if they have a great place to work at. The newer generations prefer quality of life.

One of the advantages of being virtual is that you can automate things, so automate them. Automating tasks does not make automated tasks less human—well, technically it is less human. What I mean is it does not make it less humane. People often have this notion that making it automated or robotlike diminishes the human touch. I disagree. Technology is built to make our lives easier. By making it easier on everyone involved, it makes it more humane. Less is more and more is less; make things easy.

So, how do you create an environment or culture that supports the best virtual environment?

> *Create the kind of workplace and company culture that will attract great talent. If you hire brilliant people, they will make work feel more like play.*
>
> RICHARD BRANSON, FOUNDER OF VIRGIN GROUP AND AUTHOR

ESTABLISH WORK TRADITIONS
FUN AND GAMES
One of the leaders I interviewed for this book mentioned that work needs some shenanigans from time to time.

I personally saw my company utilize this point recently. In my current project, we have twenty-two teams, with more than five hundred individuals total. To get them to interact with each other, the leadership team came up with games to boost the holiday feeling. Work traditions can build a feeling of community and make your existing one more tight knit.

We had a huge scavenger hunt game in which each agent could participate, and whichever team got the most points won the bragging rights and a gift card for each member of the winning team. To do a scavenger hunt in a virtual environment, the host provided items to look for, and the team members looked for those items in their houses and took pictures of them.

My team did not win, but it did allow everyone to show some team spirit. One of the days we asked for Christmas items. I told my team to send me all the images we had of nutcrackers. Sure enough, I received close to twenty images of a nutcracker. Small games like these increase worker interaction.

PICTURE-PICTURE
Encourage employees to share pictures of their pets, children, favorite memes, cooking skills or workstations. Even a #ThrowbackThursday picture is a fun way to keep employees engaged and connected.

HEIDI LYNNE KURTER, LEADERSHIP COACH AND WORKPLACE CULTURE CONSULTANT (KURTER, 2020)

There was this one time when our team got talking about their favorite ice cream and one member said we should do an ice cream day.

Me: "Ice cream day sounds great. Bring your favorite ice cream and we'll have ice cream or juice if you do not have ice cream."

A few days later as I was editing this book, I read the quote above from Heidi, and inspired by her, I told my team that we will do a #ThrowbackThursday. Bring your ice cream, a picture, and a story behind that picture.

During our #ThrowbackThursday event some people got to talking about their wedding anniversary, first job, first child, when they were in school, family vacation, show performances, and so on. It was great to have this with the team. One team member even said, "I like that people chose their baby photos. I will do that next time." This individual was the one who chose her wedding photo to share with us.

There was also a random day to send in any fall images that they had, and someone posted a picture of a leaf transitioning from green to red along with the caption, "I found this during my stroll yesterday." Another individual took a picture of their Halloween decor for this year and the year before. She even told us the story of why she added the ghost decor. The next day she posted a picture of her son with a pumpkin and commented that this was their first pumpkin for the season, which her dad brought for them. Another individual posted all her home decor showing us her minimalist and elegant design. Pictures are fun ways to build engagement and know more about team members.

CHANNELS
Establish more touch points in your virtual environment through ways creating channels where people can chat. In a

virtual environment, touch points are different than those in the conventional office environment. Touch points are points of contact or interactions. Meetings, one-on-ones, and accidental meetings in the hallway are examples of touch point situations. We all know work requires fun that allows everyone to reenergize.

Create separate chat channels for work and nonwork related channels. It is easy to create content and fill out the pages. You do not want to be left in a position where you have a hard time sorting through the information.

In our Slack, we have separate channels with different purposes. We have team channels where people in the team can ask questions and team members can collaborate with one another. Places, or channels, where people can talk about other things not related to work can help with building team culture; this gives them a chance to know each other on another level.

We have a random channel for anything random a team member wants to share and a positivity channel to help produce some positive vibes.

Our work is revolved around customer service. Eventually, there was a span when the customers were affecting the team members, and you could feel that spirits were down and tensions were high. To uplift and motivate people, leadership created the positivity channel, along with the question of the day channel.

In the *State of Remote Work 2019* report by Buffer, the second biggest struggle with working remotely is loneliness (Buffer, 2021).

Amir Salihefendic, CEO of Doist said, "Remote work isn't just a different way to work—it's a different way to live. And, unlike what you might see on Instagram, working remotely doesn't mean you jetset to exotic locations to drink piña coladas on the beach" (Trueman, 2020). He is right: remote work is not all fun and games, which is why we should incorporate some fun and games into work and find ways to increase worker motivation.

On a much more serious note, Amir added, "We need to acknowledge that isolation, anxiety, and depression are significant problems when working remotely, and we must figure out ways and systems to resolve these complex issues" (Trueman, 2020). This is where, as a leader, you should try to establish a great work culture.

INCLUSIVITY

> *Inclusiveness in working agreements and leading by example are key. Being remote can lead to a lot less ad-hoc collaboration and more one-on-one conversations. No one wants to spend their whole day on Zoom, so ensuring that you are keeping the spirit of collaboration and inclusiveness alive is super important. Directly asking individuals how they are feeling is a great step in the right direction.*
>
> CODY CORNELL, CO-FOUNDER AND CHIEF STRATEGY OFFICER OF SWIMLANE (FORBES TECHNOLOGY COUNCIL, 2021)

When creating content, use something that everyone can relate to; be inclusive so people can engage easily. One of my coworkers posted this in a channel: *When did you last see a sunset? Post your picture.* She got a lot of engagement since a lot of people have seen a sunset.

When in a meeting, make it your job to have all members speak. I ask what the member has been up to during the weekend or something similar. Fifteen minutes of unstructured socializing can help with increasing performance (Dugan and Bhatnagar, 2018). Ask consistently. Eventually, they will come out of their shell. The best way to get an answer without scaring people is asking a question everyone on the team can answer to, such as, "What's your favorite book?" This ensures the shy ones do not feel like they are placed under the spotlight.

In the early years of Trello, when not a lot of its workers were working remote, Trello had a town hall meeting every month to see the CEO, give demos, meet new members, and answer any questions employees had. In the beginning, when there were only twenty-two people, not everyone was remote. In New York, where Trello's headquarters are located, the New Yorkers would meet in an office while the remote people would be on the screen. They would have their town hall that way (Startupfood, 2016). Promoting an environment of inclusivity may be as easy as having people who are in the office open their PC and view the meeting through their screens.

They found out it was not the right way to do it and quickly realized it made the remote people feel like they were missing out on something, like they were excluded. The solution they came up with was to have the New Yorkers be on their computers as well. That way, they were all together doing the same thing and having the same access to the same resource (Startupfood, 2016).

SERVE AS AN EXAMPLE

Whenever I welcome a new team member, I do a shout-out: "Welcome to the team, [NEW MEMBER NAME]" and even add in emojis. One thing I noticed is people are more willing to reply and engage when someone starts the engagement.

> *Little gestures go a long way in alleviating stress or providing feedback to questions that are sometimes never even asked. Go a step further, and offer public praise in a group chat, like "Shout out to Josh for closing that deal!"*
>
> NICK KANE, MANAGING PARTNER AT JANEK PERFORMANCE GROUP AND AUTHOR OF *CRITICAL SELLING: HOW TOP PERFORMERS ACCELERATE THE SALES PROCESS AND CLOSE MORE DEALS* (KANE, 2020)

Some people fear being placed in the spotlight. So, as a leader, you need to show initiative in displaying the action you want and others will soon follow suit. Little things like these build team rapport. The more you get your team to engage, the more they become comfortable with doing things.

The other thing I had my team do is help in creating a positive work environment by, for example, posting images of their artwork. Sometimes I would randomly post songs such as "Can't Stop the Feeling" by Justin Timberlake.

REWARD THE HUNS

A person who feels appreciated will always do more than what is expected.

UNKNOWN

In the book *Leadership Secrets of Attila the Hun* by Wess Roberts, "Booty has become a powerful force that ignites the spirits of our warriors, driving them to commit their talents to any nation that bribes them into service. [Leaders] must turn this lust for booty into a more disciplined distribution of rewards to the Huns who willingly give their service to our nation either in or out of battle" (Roberts, 1987).

Appreciation can go a long way. Praising people and rewarding them for their remarkable work helps with keeping the team motivated. We have a reward system in our company in which, every week each supervisor picks the best agent of the week. The culture committee then announces the best agents of the weeks to the entire company.

At times, the committee would give prizes, such as an Amazon gift card, if the schedules were met and such. Whether the reward is material or not, make sure to reward appropriately—your team will certainly appreciate it. Logan Chierotti, founder of InternetReputation.com, mentioned it is "imperative you create systems to show your virtual team how much you appreciate their work" (Chierotti, 2017). Praise the team for a job well done. After all, who does not want to be praised?

Doing shout-outs works really well. Each time we have an onboarding process, the shadow masters, seasoned agents who help new agents, love it when I do a shout-out thanking them for helping onboard the new team members. Practicing gratitude and rewarding good behavior positively reinforces good behavior.

> *While working remotely it is important that your employees still feel valued and recognized for the hard work they are doing. Companies should consider dedicating time each week for employee recognition. Having someone on their team express gratitude and kudos for their work can help ensure employees feel like they matter and stay loyal to your company.*
>
> ALLISON BARR ALLEN, CO-FOUNDER AND COO AT FAST (FORBES TECHNOLOGY COUNCIL, 2021)

ENCOURAGE A COLLABORATIVE TEAM

Shared moments like these accumulate and contribute to a strong sense of shared identity. It's important to cultivate that same sense of belonging in when managing a virtual team, but leaders have to go about it a little more creatively.

FOND, 2021

One thing I found helpful was having my team members rely on each other. I wanted them to be independent, so even if I am not working, they can do things on their own. What I found is some of the teams in our company struggle with people answering their questions. Most of the time, they had to wait for their supervisor to get the information, even if the information was already posted in the updates channel.

Getting information in twenty to thirty minutes is not feasible, especially when you need to provide the customer the answers to their questions and concerns. I had my team collaborate with each other and share their knowledge. By doing so, even when I am in a meeting, they get helped by other members of the team. Teamwork allows the people in your team to feel safe and flourish in their tasks, knowing that other people have their backs and they are not out there to fend for themselves.

Teamwork makes the dream work.

JOHN MAXWELL, AMERICAN AUTHOR,
SPEAKER, AND PASTOR

People also like being a part of something bigger than themselves. Steve Huffman, founder and CEO of Reddit and founder of Hipmunk said that he:

> *Really appreciate how amazing people are and how incredible humanity is. And a natural byproduct of people being together is to build stuff. And one of the metaphors I like to use for Reddit is that of a city. Outside this window of San Francisco, and like, no one person designed San Francisco, or even any single part of it. But neighborhoods emerge culture emerges all of these things that you can do in a city emerge. That's how I read it. It's just an online version of humanity. I think, we want to lean into that because people do incredible things. What we've seen time and time again, is that when people like are in the right context, they actually overwhelmingly I think, do the right*

> *thing. Yep. And it's when we put constraints on them that we actually get in the way of that.*
>
> STEVE HUFFMAN, FOUNDER AND CEO OF REDDIT AND FOUNDER OF HIPMUNK (HUFFMAN, 2021)

People build. As individuals collaborate with each other, great things are born.

GIVE PEOPLE A VISION

When the team knows the end goal and mission, it will help you reach it. Allowing the team to provide their input on how to build a great work environment will motivate the team.

When people know why and what they are fighting for, they connect better to the goal. It allows people to focus and execute on what needs to be done. Tara Clements said, "Explaining the vision and mission of work to team members helps build a cohesive goal across the team and organization."

Whenever you start a project, this always comes first. By giving people the vision, it is like giving the project an identity: it allows individuals in the team to understand why they are doing the work they are doing and what that work is. From there, people will be more participative in giving ideas that allow the group to reach the goal.

By giving people the vision, you are clarifying their mission.

REACH OUT

Encourage people to break barriers. Andrew Jornod, CEO of VertexOne, said, "Creating cross-departmental projects and initiatives will bring new people together. You can also implement new traditions and virtual activities such as trivia games or lunch-and-learns to get to know each other" (Forbes Technology Council, 2021). Activities that keep people engaged can help encourage team building. I know one of the supervisors had a Karaoke Friday as one of her activities and invited everyone in the organization to join if they were interested.

Even though you are distant from each other, you can still make leaps in your relationships. For example, Mat Ishbia, the CEO of United Wholesale Mortgage, believes so strongly that work culture is important that he lives and breathes it. In his company, "Thursdays at three o'clock is the dance party, and everybody stops working at three o'clock on Thursdays. Everyone gathered in the auditorium and had a dance party, including the CEO. For him, the people are the company's greatest asset."

Mandy Schwerin, a manager at United Wholesale Mortgage, mentioned she had a family member who passed away. The death was unexpected and the immediate family members were unprepared. Most of the costs went to the funeral itself. When she went to the memorial there were no flowers, no gifts, nothing. When the family came, "there was this giant bouquet of white roses and white lilies." Not knowing who it came from, Mandy went up to check the flowers and it came from Mat, the CEO.

When Mandy went back to work, she went to the benefits department and asked if they had sent the bouquet of flowers to the funeral home. They explained they had not. "If it said it was from Mat, then it directly came from Mat." Mandy was astonished; it is "incredible considering we have seven thousand people who work for organization and Mat still knows what is happening and reached out."

For Mandy, "maintaining the culture has not been as difficult as it could be, if [she] didn't have the support from [their] CEO and all the leadership team." She mentioned that at her job they are "constantly being educated about best leadership practices."

According to a study outlined in the *Harvard Business Review*, 46 percent of remote workers said the best managers were those who checked in frequently and regularly. As the article's authors wrote: "The most successful managers are good listeners, communicate trust and respect, inquire about workload and progress without micromanaging, and err on the side of overcommunicating" (Wingard, 2020). Accessibility is great to provide to the team; get in touch with your team on a regular basis in moderation. The daily meetings I have are always optional, but the team still goes to them and loves them.

I had a conversation with one of my team members.

Agent: "It is hard to get connected with the customers in a five-minute call. I am glad that we can talk to the team during the meetings."

Me: "I am glad you like them. I was thinking of taking them out and I know I asked back then and the team said to keep it, so I kept it." ("It" being the meetings, fifteen-minute meetings during the day and the one-hour virtual open office at the end of the day.)

Agent: "Yeah, it is great especially during the pandemic where we barely talk to anyone. It is nice to get to talk to the team."

I make sure team members are building a relationship with each other and not just building a relationship with me. The meetings in which we just talk about random stuff or ask work-related questions are beneficial to have.

Bringing back Maslow's hierarchy of needs, safety is a foundational layer from which people build upon. With that in mind, there is a need to build a safe work environment so individuals can be their best selves. Once they have established that, in this case having a safe workspace, the team will be able to gain self-fulfillment and perform well in its job.

No one wants to work in a negative environment no matter how big the pay is. People will eventually leave a bloodsucking environment. So introduce a way to allow others to feel comfortable within the virtual workspace. The information I have listed are suggestions and not prescriptions. Allow creativity and strategic planning to help you create a culture of safety, goodwill, and happiness.

KNOWLEDGE NUGGETS:

- **Establish Work traditions.** Look for something that all team members will share. Traditions are something we all can share and talk about.
- **Inclusivity.** Make people feel welcome, and give them a nudge to speak every now and then.
- **Serve as an example.** Show others what you want by exemplifying what you want them to follow.
- **Reward the Huns.** Give appreciation when appropriate.
- **Encourage a Collaborative Team.** Two heads are better than one and people will appreciate a more responsive team.
- **Give People a Vision.** Give people something to fight for together.
- **Reach Out.** Allow people to mix and intermingle so they will feel less isolated and build relationships.

CHAPTER 11

THE GUARDIAN

Google's performance management strategy is rooted in a desire to use data and analytics. Growth mindset is emphasized in the approach to employee coaching, whereby managers learn to focus on being open to the entire potential of the employee and to assume that there is always room for growth

DERLER, SANDERS, AND STEEL, 2019

The leader serves as a map and compass to those one leads. It guides them to the lost city.

Most of the people in the leadership team are high performers—that is how they got there. I find laissez-faire leadership works best for leaders who are also leading a leadership team. In the laissez-faire method, the leader tends to leave the employees alone and have them do what they need to do, helping them if they ask or need it. It is a hands-off approach to leadership, which works great in allowing creativity to flourish.

For teams that are not in leadership positions, you get the diverse range of performers—some great, some not so great. The not-so-great ones require you to handhold them a bit. This generally applies to entry level managers. This is also part of the business hierarchy, where things tend to be more menial. Hence, very little gray area or creativity is needed. When you coach someone the first time around, you will need to do most of the work.

More often, remote leadership training gets shifted to online video course such as Udemy, Coursera, LinkedIn Learning, or in-house training videos. I will be honest, sometimes I blank out when I am watching training videos. Knowing that I do that, others will most likely do that as well. Sometimes videos are not the best to learn from, especially if you struggle a lot with computers. In a virtual environment, sometimes it is best to get an actual person to train you for a period of time.

Part of coaching is differentiating ways on how people learn. So, provide a variety of mediums for your training. I prefer a mix of video plus human interaction. In my team, when they have technical issues, I send them links to multiple resources on how to fix the system issues, such as: videos, pictures, and documents containing the troubleshooting instructions.

> *Leadership coach who can provide "office hours" for your managers to sign-up for a thirty-minute slot, they can serve as a helpful spot-check and counsel on tough issues.*
>
> CLAIRE LEW, CEO OF KNOW YOUR TEAM (LEW, 2020)

The human aspect comes when the team member just cannot figure out or is having a hard time understanding the documents or videos. There are some people who find it easier to learn when there is an instructor with them. A quick Zoom video with the team member can help with this; simply do one-on-one remote coaching. When I go on a Zoom with them, I have them share their screen and let them know where and what to click.

COACHING PHASE
Your goal is not to disable them; your goal is to enable them. Empower them to be a productive contributor to society.

Micromanagement does not help in making an individual independent. The funny thing about micromanagement is your team members become so reliant on what you think is right and wrong that they cannot seem to use their own judgement of what is right or wrong. People want to do well at their jobs: allow them the opportunity to do so. No one is perfect, so allow people to make mistakes and correct them along the way. Give them accountability and ingrain this into your team's habit. As a coach, you are responsible in enhancing their skills, and accountability helps with this.

THREE MENTOR PHASE
Responsibility percentage:

FIRST PHASE: 25 PERCENT THEM, 75 PERCENT YOU
When I have someone to train, I show them first how to do it. I do the tasks myself and my mentee watches me do the work.

During this phase, your mentee will have some questions, so answer them as they go. This phase is the introduction phase; it allows you to introduce new concepts to the individual without overwhelming them. If you take the reins, you have more control of what they are learning.

The first phase is great when someone just joins the team. When people are learning how to use software to navigate the virtual environment, the team member will need you more during this phase. One thing that will fully differentiate the in-office environment and the virtual environment is the learning curve on how to use basic equipment.

In an in-office environment, your basic tools will be pen, paper, and mouth, and you can work with that. In a virtual environment, if you do not know how to open a chat box, then you will not be able to work. Even if you have notes on your desk, you will have a hard time sharing the information unless you type it up or show it via chat or photo. This phase is the most significant when you are working in geographically distant environment.

SECOND PHASE: 50 PERCENT THEM, 50 PERCENT YOU
During the second phase, you will be the one asking them what they should do. I still perform the task; however, I ask my mentee what steps I should do next, correcting and encouraging them along the way. This gives them the opportunity to think independently and learn how to do some complex thinking.

The second phase is less work than the first one, and your team member will still need help from time to time. This phase is usually when people get momentum in learning.

THIRD PHASE: 75 PERCENT THEM, 25 PERCENT YOU

The third phase is what I love the most. This is where you will get the feel of where your mentee is in terms of knowledge and skills. During this stage, you will have them steer the wheel themselves. You are there to answer any questions along the way.

In this phase, you can replicate the process. In my work, when we have five people join the team all at once, it takes at least a week to get people introduced to using the software. It then takes a few more weeks to get them more in tuned with using it. Phase three is the phase when you can actually ask the team member to help another team member. By doing so, you are allowing them to validate their learnings.

If you have someone on your team who is proficient in the task, you can have them be the coach starting in the first phase. The great thing about these phases is that they are replicable, so replicate.

In an environment where you need to teach people constantly, the mentoring phases are very helpful. The learning curve is steeper when the environment is new, especially if it's something you cannot physically touch. For example, software is two-dimensional: unless you are one of the computer engineers who know how to take apart the software, you will have a hard time understanding what is happening.

If things are physical and you want to understand them more, you can just touch and feel the texture or break it apart piece by piece to examine it. Physical objects are easier to break apart; you can just use a hammer to do that. If you want to break software, you need a deeper understanding of computer systems. So, in a virtual space where people are not that familiar, it is always a good way to have multiple people be comfortable to teach how the software works.

As you've noticed, that mentorship/coaching is a gradual thing. Of course, you do not need to do these steps for every single thing they need help with. You will only need to do this type of training for the major tasks your team member is responsible for. For some tasks, such as fixing technical issues, you can give them a protocol to follow so they can solve it themselves. If they are unable to do so, you can hop in and help them. This teaches them independence.

One thing I like about the three mentor phase process is that it can be replicated. I use the same process for my veterans (team members who have been on the project longer than others and know how to work the system). By allowing team members to teach other team members, it becomes a way for them to strengthen their understanding of the concept. Like Phil Collins would say, "In learning you will teach, and in teaching you will learn." By teaching, they are reinforcing the lessons for themselves.

You will have to invest in your team members initially. The more you give them the necessary resources to be successful, the easier it will be for everyone involved in the long run. From what I observe on teams that do not do this initial investment, they are less productive. As more problems arise in the future, they end up fixing things and patching them up like a Band-Aid. Without curing the problem, you will end up in this Band-Aid cycle.

After you have successfully finished the three mentor phase process, you will still have to continually coach your team members; at this point it will be very minimal. If they steer off the path you want them to take, then simply steer them back to the path. Coaching will be most helpful for companies that are growing and welcoming new members. You will learn that new team members are new to the virtual environment. It is your responsibility to help them understand the new environment they are in.

To lead people walk behind them.
LAO TZU, CHINESE PHILOSOPHER AND WRITER

Help them without disabling them. In the first phase, most of them will rely heavily on you, the leader. At this point, most of your responsibility will involve equipping them with the right tools, such as documents, applications, and so on. You are also training them during this phase. Phase two involves equal sharing of the responsibility. This usually occurs when they are still becoming independent and have some sort of dependence on you. This is an interdependent relationship. Phase three is when they are independent and still need you to update them with any information you got from the corporate ladder. The idea really is for you to coach them first. Then, they coach themselves and still have access to you for questions. Then they teach others, because teaching others reinforces the information.

Coaching may mainly affect middle management or entry level management, where they are directly in charge of the people. For companies that use their own software, navigating it may be hard on their members. The leaders have to teach and train team members to learn how to fix the issues. Computer issues are harder to fix for some, especially for those who are technology averse.

One thing I learned is to not necessarily tell them what to do, but to have them directly do it themselves—this creates muscle memory. This relates to what they call practice makes perfect. Similar to *The Karate Kid*, where Jackie Chan teaches his student to clean by wiping the windows and sweeping the floor and then says to use the same movements for karate. Muscle memory comes in handy. This is the polishing of techniques from *The Book of Five Rings (Gorin No Sho): The Real Art of Japanese Management* by Musashi, Miyamoto (Musashi, 1982).

For example, in the company I work at, we use VMware, a virtual desktop or screen that is a computer within a computer. The software unfortunately glitches from time to time. I had a team member who was struggling to fix the issue inside VMware. I had to tell him to click this and click that and had to repeat it three times for him to build the memory of what he should be doing to fix the issue. A document that contains instructions on how to fix it may not be sufficient.

At first, especially with a new team, I find it better to use a servant leadership type of approach. You really need to show the team how to navigate and fix the problems. Some team members at first find it difficult to navigate virtually. Over time, they grow more acquainted with the systems.

Zoom screen sharing is good for coaching. Sometimes when you have an individual experiencing some technical difficulties, you can use screen takeover to show them how to fix the issue on the spot. You can also do a screen share with them and direct them on how to troubleshoot issues. Most of the remote work is knowledge work, not menial; most of the coaching happens in the beginning. Once everyone gets used to how things work, there is no need to do as much work later.

BUDDY-BUDDY SYSTEM

Give each new team member a buddy or an accountability partner.

65 percent consider coaching by peers as important or very important activities.

DERLER, SANDERS, AND STEEL, 2019

Back when Alex Stieb, serial entrepreneur, investor, and father of five, was a Boy Scout becoming an Eagle Scout, he learned about the buddy system. He explained when they went out to go on canoe trips or swim on a lake, they always had a buddy with them. The purpose of the buddy was to make sure that when they went out on a trip they would come back safely, and they always had a board check-in and checkout. The buddy system allowed the scouts to get a helping hand and have an accountability partner.

In Alex's company, there were teams of two or three when he implemented a simple but effective buddy system. The buddies have the responsibility to check in with teams on a frequent basis, ensuring regular conversations and interaction.

Alex tries to take the highest performers of the team and group them with lower performers to balance out his teams.

He takes "the leader of the highest performing team and put them with the lowest performing crew, and then put the lowest performing crew with the highest performing team." His teams get swapped occasionally, "and what that ends up doing is it counterbalances, so that way you have a better leader in charge of lesser [performing] teams" and rotate once in a while to decrease stagnation. The buddy system is helpful especially to members who are struggling at work.

It allows other members to keep up with their action items. According to Rodolphe Dutel, founder of Remotive and former director of operations at Buffer, Buffer also pairs their people with buddies (Startupfood, 2015).

My leadership style at its core is connected to my *ikigai*, a reason for being, my life purpose, which is to influence others to be the best version of themselves. The quote that has always influenced my *ikigai* is: "Give a man a fish, feed him for a day. Teach the man how to fish, feed him for a lifetime." This has greatly influenced my leadership style.

In the beginning, I start off with the servant leadership style, as I try to help team members maneuver around their roles. This is phase one (75 percent me and 25 percent them) as they grow and develop to become independent and sure of themselves. Like a mother bird, I set them free to fly on their own. All throughout their journey, I use a transformational leadership style.

The funny thing about influence is if you can influence a person to perform in ways that are beneficial to them and others, you allow for an easier transition to grow without the necessary structure built around it. Their self-accountability is the thing that creates the structure.

Give them some tough love sometimes. By allowing intellectual stimulation, you are providing them a space for growth.

It is your obligation to develop the individual. It will require participation from the individual as well. Realize that when people are not performing to the set standards, they are either lazy or in need of some additional mentoring. It is up to you as the leader to determine which it is. Rehabilitation must take place before things turn for the worst. I always tell my team what is expected of them and will let them know if they fall below the expectation. I then help them get back on track. Now, if the person is falling behind after you have taught them, then it might be that they are just not a good fit for the role. It is work after all; it is not all roses.

PEER COACHING IMPROVES GOODWILL

> *Everyone can coach. Every person in your organization can communicate with others and can challenge them to lift their game, encourage them to see new possibilities, confront them with their own potential, affirm their many talents, and remind them of how great it feels to do extraordinary work.*
>
> GREGG THOMPSON, AUTHOR OF *THE MASTER COACH: LEADING WITH CHARACTER, BUILDING CONNECTIONS, AND ENGAGING IN EXTRAORDINARY CONVERSATIONS* (THOMPSON, 2021)

A survey of US full-time workers found that peer coaching is beneficial long term. Over 65 percent of workers are fulfilled when they are regularly engaging in peer coaching. Seventy-three percent also felt a stronger sense of belonging (Hurst, 2020).

Peer coaching is a way to reduce remote work-related stress.

Peer-to-peer help allows team members to spend time with each other. It helps especially well with team collaboration. Aaron Hurst, CEO and co-founder of Imperative and author of *The Purpose Economy*, said that peers "listen and talk equally, and support and encourage each other's vulnerability" (Hurst, 2020). It helps with stress reduction and improves overall team cooperation. It allows members to implement their learning and validate its efficacy.

> *Peer coaching is a confidential process through which two or more colleagues work together to reflect on current practices; expand, refine, and build new skills; share ideas; teach one another; conduct classroom research; or solve problems in the workplace.*
>
> ROBBINS, 1991 (GOVINDARAJU, 2021)

Peer coaching is like killing two birds with one stone. On one hand, the peer coach is learning leadership skills, and on the other hand, the other team member is learning, and the last advantage is that this can be replicated. In the virtual environment where a buddy system is helpful, integrating peer coaching in your team is beneficial and fosters teamwork.

PARENTING STYLES AS LEADERSHIP STYLES

Leadership is like parenting; you do not want to want to overprotect your child nor be too permissive.

FOUR PARENTING STYLES

AUTHORITARIAN

Authoritarian parents "are obedience-and status-oriented, and expect their orders to be obeyed without explanation" according to Baumrind (Cherry, 2020). This type of parenting style values obedience and often resorts to punishment if the child does not fulfill the expectations. Lack of explanation as to why the rules are implemented characterizes this style. This results in children associating obedience and success with love, having low self-esteem, happiness, and social competence.

I have a colleague who practices an authoritarian style. From what I gather, doing an authoritarian style of leading your team can cause lower retention. More often than not, mainly because if they do not meet her expectations, she is ready to let them go. Though this approach is often seen in a negative light, there will be times when authoritarian leadership style will be useful, especially during a crisis when the company needs a firmer approach.

AUTHORITATIVE

The authoritative parenting style provides expectations backed by support and guidance. The parent is more forgiving when it comes to mistakes and takes the time to make the child understand why they were punished. This style is more democratic and nurturing. Authoritative parents "monitor and impart clear standards for their children's conduct. They are assertive but not intrusive and restrictive. Their disciplinary methods are supportive, rather than punitive. They want their children to be assertive as well as socially responsible, and self-regulated as well as cooperative," said Baumrind (Cherry, 2020). Children raised in this style of parenting tend to be more happy, self-confident, and have good social skills.

The authoritative style is more useful than all other styles when it comes to coaching and leading the team. For example, when I told my team that, although they can pick the time they want to work, they are expected to come when they are scheduled. If the customers want 270 full-time hours completed to do the job, we need to meet those expectations; otherwise, we could lose the contract.

They could still change their schedules; they just needed to show up for the time they scheduled their work. By explaining it to them, the team had a high level of self-accountability and reduced absence and lateness. I think this parenting style connects well with the concept of "tough love"—give them expectations to follow and the support necessary to flourish.

These are the qualities of an authoritative leader:

> *Authoritative leaders, also called visionary leaders, tend to approach leadership like a mentor guiding a mentee. Instead of telling their team to follow instructions and do as they say, authoritative leaders put themselves in the scenario and utilize a "come with me" approach. They have a firm understanding of the challenges to overcome and the goals to reach, and*

> have a clear vision for achieving success. Authoritative leaders inspire motivation. They offer direction, guidance, and feedback.
>
> TIM STOBIERSKI, MARKETING SPECIALIST AND CONTRIBUTING WRITER FOR HARVARD BUSINESS SCHOOL ONLINE (STOBIERSKI, 2019)

PERMISSIVE

The permissive parenting style has low expectations. They are indulgent to their children and "are more responsive than they are demanding. They are nontraditional and lenient, do not require mature behavior, allow considerable self-regulation, and avoid confrontation," said Baumrind (Cherry, 2021). Children tend to have issues with authority and are low in happiness and self-regulation.

UNINVOLVED

Uninvolved parenting is characterized by low demands and responsiveness toward their child. They are neglectful and detached from the child's life (Cherry, 2020). Children of the uninvolved parenting style tend to be less competent and have low self-esteem and self-control (Cherry, 2014). Both permissive and uninvolved are bad ways of leading. In the workplace, there seems to be this notion that people will directly do what they are supposed to do without the necessary training involved.

It is like throwing your baby into the pool hoping that instincts will kick in—no pun intended—and the child will survive on its own. At times, it works fine; other times, it does not work. Some individuals who are in leadership positions do this, expecting great results. If the result is not what they expected, they are ready to get rid of the employee. It is quite absurd to place your expectations on others without training them on how to do the job or giving them the necessary expectations or tools to do the job.

WHAT MAKES AN AUTHORITATIVE LEADER BEST AT REMOTE COACHING?

Authoritative leaders provide enough handholding to help team members when transitioning to the virtual environment. If it is in the office, you can still get to work by being physically at work. In a virtual environment, they may require one to get on a system to indicate that they are clocked in. How to use an app or a website is not something that one can learn immediately; it requires a steeper learning curve. The authoritative leader also provides enough empowerment for people grow professionally and personally. The ability of the authoritative leader to provide assistance and to allow the person to fly on their own is a combination that is necessary for the proper transitioning from in-office to virtual.

Svetlana Whitener, emotional intelligence executive coach at InLight Coaching, said the "root of an 'authoritarian' style is power, and the root of an 'authoritative' style is empathy. A leader operates from a place of empathy (authoritative approach) he or she consistently focuses on the other person's needs and tries to be as nurturing as possible" (Whitener, 2019). The key here is to focus on the need of the team member and nurture them, and by doing so the leader is helping the individual flourish. Svetlana added that the authoritative leadership approach helps build confidence and allows the mentee to foster full potential realization.

THE IMPORTANCE OF EMPATHY AND BEING CRYSTAL CLEAR

EMPATHY
The authoritative leader nurtures goodwill among everyone involved. Tim Stobierski, marketing specialist and contributing writer for Northeastern University, said understanding the team member's emotions, desires, and worries, personal or professional, helps the authoritative leader to better "identify potential roadblocks to performance and remove them, while simultaneously incentivizing success" (Stobierski, 2019). Empathy then is a necessity for leading using the authoritative leadership approach.

When people think of coaching, they always think of something that is direct—the person constantly being there for the person—but coaching can also be indirect.

BE CRYSTAL CLEAR
Authoritative leaders bring clarity. Tim says an authoritative leader has the ability to "inspire, motivate, and influence," and this allows them to be effective in connecting with their team (Stobierski, 2019).

The authoritative leader has the ability to make corporate goals be communicated in a way that is easy for employees to understand and follow. Understanding is key to ensuring everyone is aligned to the organization's goal. Remember the issue the project had about scheduling? I explained to my team the importance of aligning with the schedule and explaining why it is important to the contract to each worker in the team. Most of the time, the team does align with the schedule and very rarely will they veer off the schedule.

The authoritative leader brings direction. The leader has a clarity of vision and knows how to get there. During the process, they also provide "constructive feedback as they work toward organizational goals," according to Tim (Stobierski, 2019). Providing a pathway for people to follow to reach their destination increases effectiveness and efficiency for goal achievement. Part of providing direction is the comfort it brings to the team members. If they know what they are doing is what was directed, they are more comfortable in following through with what they are currently doing.

For the most part, you will end up using a mixture of all of the parenting styles. They do, after all, have different contributions to the workplace. Authoritative leadership, however, may very well be a great style to use in a remote setting.

I strive to have my team be made of independent individuals. My leadership style is malleable, starting at servant leadership and going to transformational leadership. I want to rock people's worlds, not rock their world in a celebratory manner. But I want to rock their world as in to challenge their beliefs, so they can transform from being a caterpillar to a butterfly (metamorphosis).

I give them enough direct assistance to continue for the day, but not too much direct assistance—it makes them lazy and not work for it themselves. I give them extra to boost motivation once in a while. I want them to become independent thinkers and productive beings of society, and, perhaps through them, I can make the world a little bit better.

Not all of us end up finding mentors: maybe we find them in books or among the people we encounter in life. The question is, if you are a leader, will you be that person to your team member? Coaching really is not fixed on coaching others on how to do their job but coaching them on how to think and act in ways that will be beneficial to them.

In my team, knowing that some of the individuals are college students and recent graduates, some of them have yet to build their work ethic and soft skills. I had to search for ways on how to resolve such issues. This knowledge can help them in their current work. If I can teach them something they can take as a life lesson, then I will.

I am not forward with when I try to influence the team's behaviors; I slowly convert them to doing certain tasks that can help them perform the task. Refer back to *The Karate Kid* story.

Mentoring is an interesting practice. You are taking a person under your wing and teaching them how to soar on their own. Allow mistakes to happen and for others to learn from them. Teach the student to become the teacher.

KNOWLEDGE NUGGETS:
- **Three Mentor Phase**
  - **First Phase: 25 Percent Them, 75 Percent You.** Leader carries a heavier role as mentee adjusts to the role.
  - **Second Phase: 50 Percent Them, 50 Percent You.** Leader and mentee split the role.
  - **Third phase: 75 Percent Them, 25 Percent You.** Mentee will now take the lead while the leader is available for needed assistance or guidance.
- **Buddy-Buddy System.** Pair the new member with a team member who will help them while they adjust.
- **Peer Coaching Improves Goodwill.** Peer coaching allows the person teaching to strengthen their knowledge about the topics, while the student learns as well. Peer coaching allows the team members to have time to spend to get to know each other and build rapport.
- **Parenting Styles**
  - **Authoritarian.** Will dictate to others what needs to be done.
  - **Authoritative.** Provides guidance and coaching.
  - **Permissive.** Lenient and not demanding.
  - **Uninvolved.** Low responsiveness and Neglectful.
- **What Makes an Authoritative Leader Best at Remote Coaching?** Giving a helping hand and empowering people is a combination that is great to exercise with remote workers.
- **The Importance of Empathy and Being Crystal Clear**
  - **Empathy.** Know team members' weaknesses and strengths and accommodate their growth based on the information.
  - **Be Crystal Clear.** If people know what you want, they will know what results to deliver.

PART III

SEEING BEYOND

CHAPTER 12

FUTURE OF REMOTE WORK

―

BRING! I lift my arm, searching for my phone to turn off the alarm. I swing my legs off the bed, shift myself into a sitting position, and stand up. Opening my bedroom door, I walk six steps forward, toward the bathroom. I take a bath under the steaming hot shower, then brush my teeth to prepare for the workday.

I stretch my hand, taking hold of the hanger, and unbutton my long-sleeve collared shirt to wear. I still have to be presentable at work.

I do work from home, but it's not much different from an in-office setting. I still need to make myself presentable. And like most of the remote workers, I wear my pajamas for my bottoms. Why not, right? They only see half of me on Zoom—just one of the perks of working from home.

I turn on my laptop, move my mouse to open Safari, and type in Slack. My computer auto-populates the search bar, and I click enter. After a few magical seconds, I am now at work. This is my daily commute. Not much, I know. This is one of the advantages of working remotely.

WELCOME TO REMOTE WORK

> *The convenience of working from home simply cannot be rivaled, and it continues to be the primary workspace choice for remote and independent professionals. In fact, most office-optional professionals spend upwards of four days working from home each week.*
>
> DARREN BUCKNER, CEO OF WORKFROM (BUFFER, 2019)

MISCONCEPTIONS ABOUT REMOTE WORKERS

When you think of remote work, you think of people working in their pajamas with little to no supervision, people messing around, and questionable worker productivity. In reality, when work goes remote, such as what happened in 2020, remote work was not offered as an option, it became an absolute must.

> *The virus has broken through cultural and technological barriers that prevented remote work in the past, setting in motion a structural shift in where work takes place.*
>
> MCKINSEY & COMPANY, 2020

People think everyone loves to work remotely, but that is not entirely the case. Some people I interviewed expressed some of their anxieties about having to work remotely. Imagine being launched to the moon with little notice, minimal instructions, and scarce resources at hand. That is what happened in 2020; people were launched into a virtual workforce at lightning speed.

A survey conducted by Buffer about where remote workers primarily work from shows 84 percent responded that they work from home, followed by co-working locations at 8 percent, then coffee shops and cafes at 4 percent (Buffer, 2019). Remote workers do not work entirely from home, and some prefer places that may have traffic available, such as coffee shops and co-working locations.

When work was launched from a collocated space to a virtual workspace, others were concerned about working remotely. Some workers had never worked remotely before; thoughts about the lack of routines that help an individual be a productive worker, lack of office space, sharing space with everyone at home, and isolation became concerns.

The virtual environment is one that is full of anxiety and stress, as life and work merge and morph together. Yet remote work has its own unique quality that people come to love: the lack of the morning commute, the joy of a more flexible work time, and the ability to be everywhere.

FORCEFUL REINTRODUCTION OF REMOTE WORK

The COVID-19 pandemic introduced a massive trial for working virtually. Work that was thought to be impossible to do remotely is now thriving in the virtual environment. Most of the virtual work tended to be knowledge-based, so understandably, not all jobs are able to do this. As years go and lifestyles develop, more and more companies will have to transition from in-office to virtual settings.

Most jobs that can be moved to remote are mostly knowledge-based jobs and not physical labor jobs, so unless robots are used, it will still take us time to move to being fully remote.

Some of the people I interviewed during the research of this book were ready to move back to the conventional office style. Mind you, at that time there was a national lockdown and gatherings were minimal, which encourages the want to go back to the office to see other people. Adding another layer into consideration through this reaction, one can observe how humans are social creatures from the get-go. We want to have that connection with others.

Looking at the future prospects, we have encountered how beneficial it is to work virtually. Yet, there is still part of the workforce that is eager to go back to the office. Several of the individuals I interviewed, after the nine months of trial run for remote work, want to go back to the in-office setting.

Robin Mishik-Jett, director of operations and my former co-worker, said, "Companies today automatically think everyone knows how to use Zoom, Skype, Teams, Outlook via the web, Outlook for desktop, Google Meet ups, [and] etc." Because of a heavy work schedule, there was no time for her to set aside to learn how to use new technology. Robin was frustrated and added, "Employers have to have systems in place to help the less technical. It can't be a given that everyone knows how to use everything, especially working remotely without guidance and support." Robin did get her tech issues sorted out with the help of her husband, who has experience in tech.

For others, "the challenge is that the average person has not been able to optimize their work to their advantage. The process is often too complex and has required IT at every turn. The time and the cost to deliver it has been too long. So, people have settled for the old way of working," said Mark Mader, president and CEO of Smartsheet (Wu, 2020). Others have a hard time adjusting to environmental tools that have a steeper learning curve and would prefer doing things the old way.

For others it is simply because humans are social creatures.

People miss other people and sometimes the virtual office is not enough to allow us that physical form of human connection: hugs or a simple handshake.

INTEREST IN REMOTE WORK

In survey conducted by Blind, an anonymous career-related post app, on companies such as Amazon, Google, Apple, Microsoft, JP Morgan, Facebook, and Goldman Sachs, workers were asked if they preferred to get a yearly $30,000 raise or choose to permanently work from home.

Approximately two-thirds of the respondents chose to work from home:

> About 64 percent of Amazon workers who answered the question preferred permanent work from home, as well as 62 percent of Microsoft employees and 67 percent of Google employees. Apple employees would

> *rather take permanent work from home over $30,000 more at 69 percent, and Salesforce employees at 76 percent.*
>
> JACK KELLY, CEO, FOUNDER, AND EXECUTIVE RECRUITER (KELLY, 2021)

Jack Kelly said after looking at the opportunity cost lost if they do not work remotely, such as losing time to have "hobbies, have a side gig, break away to play some golf, read a book, watch your kids' soccer games or just enjoy and savor the extra hours you used to have" (Kelly, 2021), people just preferred to work remotely.

After considering the advantages such as being in comfy work-from-home clothes, less commute time, being able to do some house chores, and maybe spending time with family, it was more beneficial for the workers to work from home.

CHALLENGES IN REMOTE WORK

ISOLATION

One aspect that can be a bummer when doing remote work is how you can easily isolate yourself. I, unfortunately, have the tendency to isolate from my colleagues. When I started as an agent, I barely interacted with people in Slack, which was what we were using as our communication tool. I only answered when needed and refrained from participating when not necessary.

When I became a supervisor, I did not intentionally isolate myself from other supervisors. I was fairly communicative with my teams, so I never thought I was "siloing" from the rest of the leadership team. I did have the tendency to focus on my work and make everything around me nonexistent. In this case, my full attention was on my team for whom I am responsible. Luckily, my supervisor kept bringing me out to be more participatory. I started to spend more time with other supervisors. He did his job as a leader; he pulled me out of my silo.

Social isolation can happen easily. All the meetings I have for my team were optional before I switched it to a conditional one. I found out some of the team members were not coming to the meeting at all and were not interacting with the rest of the team members.

Upon finding this out, I shifted my meeting to a conditional one, providing the option of two meetings, one at 12:30 p.m. and one at 3:30 p.m. Team members who were full-time needed to attend one of them. If one could not come to the meeting at 12:30, then they needed to come at 3:30. The individuals who were not talking to the team members started to come to the meetings, getting more exposure, and eventually they got the hang of talking to others. Once they were more comfortable, I switched it back to optional.

As leaders, you need to care for the mental and emotional health of those you lead. It really comes down to taking care of what Robin Sharma, Canadian writer of *The Monk Who Sold His Ferrari*, would call as the four interior empires of an individual: heartset, healthset, soulset, and mindset.

Allow space for fun. After all, we are not well-oiled machines that start ticking the moment the clock starts.

RELATIONSHIP BUILDING

Relationship building is important, because without it, collaborating and connecting with others will be difficult.

Ana Simpson was a cross-country manager who led her remote team when she was in Romania, with teams reporting from Greece and Bulgaria. Ana said there was a time when she needed to fly to where her remote employees were located to build and enhance her relationships with them, gaining an authentic connection.

The team had a hard time during the transition to remote work. Ana "could sense that nothing was being established"; they had a hard time transitioning as they had their doubts about her: "Who is she?" they would ask. "She doesn't speak our language" (though both sides did speak English) and "She doesn't understand the specifics of the country."

As they were struggling, Ana decided to visit there every week so they could see her next to them. She did this to show she was there for them: "I'm here in the middle of your problems," so they could adjust better.

At times, when teams are down, the necessity to see the team personally may arise. Eventually, a mixture of physical and virtual may arise in terms of remote work arrangements. Collocated or workplace hubs may increase.

BURNOUT

One of the issues that comes with remote work is working overtime and causing burnout. I found this in some of my colleagues who had a hard time turning off from work. One told me that even if he was not clocked in, he would come to Slack and see what others were posting.

During a power outage in Texas, another coworker would be on her phone, answering other people's questions. I do think she loves to work, because even if she is absent, she still answers questions in the team channel.

I personally think people need time off from work and should turn off work mode from time to time. I never had an issue with this since I have created a line between work and life. Work is part of my life, but it is not my entire life.

At times when I overwork, even thinking becomes a difficult task at the end of the day. There is this fog that is clouding my mind, making thinking a tedious task. When it comes to days like these, a good rest is my only remedy.

Now this subject is subjective and will depend on the individual if they want to spend more hours working. I do prefer if people take the time to take care of themselves so they can be more prepared for the next workday. I like to get some downtime and focus on the other aspect of my life, such as writing this book, other random projects I have, learning, and spending time with family.

ZOOMER GENERATION

The next workforce, Millennials and Generation Z, are highly in tune with technology. The digital nomad population was found to have increased of 2.5 million from the previous year. Research in 2019 by MBO Partners found that over 7.3

million Americans workers describe themselves as digital nomads (MBO Partners, 2021).

There was one team member that kept flying from Virginia to Dallas and vice versa. One month he is in Dallas, the next he is in Virginia. The ability to travel around the States during a working season has never been easier. I like working remotely, mainly for convenience. Commuting cost (money and time) is highly reduced. I remember having to spend another hour when I commuted. With that gone, I can get an extra hour of sleep or an extra hour to do something else.

Ian Siegel, CEO and co-founder of ZipRecruiter, said millennials value "salary, flexibility of work schedule, and then location" (Wu, 2020). The shift in values got the employers to fight among each other to grab the talent they try to recruit. Ian added, "Employers are finding themselves offering that as a benefit, that flexibility of remote work, set your own work hours and location" (Wu, 2020). Tara Clements told me when she was "talking to friends and peers recently, most wouldn't consider taking a new job if they didn't offer remote work or flexibility." The change in accommodation offerings is a telltale sign of the shifting working environment. To add on to the interest, technology is moving fast toward making it easier and more accessible to work online.

One thing that can be addressed about future leadership is that people now should start looking at how to lead Generation Z, since they will be the next workforce. Daniel Goleman, psychologist, author, and science journalist, published an article about how a "generation has spoken." Generation Z has identified themselves as purpose driven, purchasing from companies based on what they stand for. Consumer habits help one better understand a population, which in this case is Generation Z (Goleman, 2021).

So the question is, how, as a leader, should you lead a Gen Zer? "While purpose has long been linked to retention and engagement, I would argue that when it comes to Gen Z, it's actually a critical component of getting new talent in the door" (Goleman, 2021). This adds to another layer of how you should lead virtually, since in the near future, employees will be Gen Zers.

My seventeen-year-old told me that her generation (Gen Z) is now being known as the Zoomers. (Like the Boomers—the generation where Zoom took over our whole lives!)

SHANNON ROBERTS, CEO & EOS IMPLEMENTER (ROBERST, 2021)

In the near future, remote or virtual work will increase—will there be a full 100 percent scale remote work force? Not in the near future. Companies will come to adopt the ability to be malleable, depending on what the worker wants. Will it be remote or conventional office? It will for sure be a mix of both. There will be a rise of collocated workspaces where people can easily come and go, whenever they want.

The COVID-19 pandemic did not introduce remote work; it increased the pace of its integration into the workforce. As an increase of a virtual lifestyle arises, there is greater need for remote leaders: How to connect with others from afar. How to create a workspace that can be less intimidating and more nurturing and fun. Your soft skills and tech skills will surely be challenged when you start working remotely. Hone your skills and help your team be a success.

All I can say is welcome to the Zoomer Generation.

ACKNOWLEDGMENTS

I would like to express my gratitude to the following individuals who supported me in this endeavor and made it a possibility to bring about the creation of this book. Thank you for the support!

Mary Claryns Truz
Mary Claire Truz
Kellan Kyros Truz
Rizaldy Truz
Victoria Truz
Kaitlyn Wineteer
Dan Drew
Benjamin Wargo
Robin Mishik-Jett
Max Eleftherio
Keanani Chaco
Kent Christian Lanurias
Laura Koch
Mary Diaz
Tryphena Koomson
Stephanie Yamauchi
Santos Gracias
Emily Oh
Salah Mohammed
Waseema Khan
N. Gorine
Payton Lynch
Amena Jamali
Eric Koester
Cierra R. Branch
Roy Dugayo
Agnieszka Rostkowski
Amanuel Yiblet
Mandy Schwerin
Tara Clements
Jamie Jay
Sr. Mary Angelica

Traci Baird
Kelly Barrett
Christopher Tam
Jennifer Davis
Ana Simpson

Stan Murzyn
Alex Stieb
Mark Bundang
Adrian Ward

I wrote this book not knowing the arduous process ahead, so without further ado, I give thanks to the following individuals who have helped make this process a little bit easier and made this dream a reality:

To Professor Koester, who triggered this entire HURRAH to happen, thank you for showing me the path to be a creator. To the Creator Institute team, New Degree Press team, thank you. To my editors, Dierdre Hammons, Janice Riley, Amanda Brown, Caroline Coggan, and Vladimir Dudas, who have been patient with me (especially Janice), thank you. To Kristy Carter, my wrangler, thank you. To Gjorgji Pejkovski and the cover design team, thank you. To Tara Clements, Stephanie Yamauchi, Robin Misik-Jett, and Sr. Mary Angelica, for sharing with me your thoughts, thank you. To the beta readers, thank you. To the sculptor team, the main reason why I wrote about this topic, thank you.

To my family who supported and helped me throughout this process, thank you: Mama, Papa, Ate Claire, Kellan, and special thanks to my sister Mary Claryns. Ate Claire, for your nursing insights, thank you. To my family, thank you for taking care of me, being patient, and giving me the space to write this book. Your moral support is forever appreciated.

To Claryns, thank you for being a great cheerleader and inspiring me along the way. Your assistance was an excellent contribution to making the book come to life. Your continuous belief has equipped me with the strength to carry on this trek. Thank you, Yen.

Thank you to those I did not mention who helped me make this book. I believe throughout one's life we are constantly developing. So to those who helped me develop for the better, up to this point and in the future, know that you are truly appreciated. Thank you.

APPENDIX

BRIEF HISTORY AND REVAMP OF VIRTUAL WORK

Allied. "The History of Telecommuting." Accessed August 16, 2021. https://www.alliedtelecom.net/the-history-of-telecommuting/.

Boulder, Colo. "Global Workplace Analytics & FlexJobs Report 159 Percent Increase in Remote Work Since 2005." Cision PRWeb. July 30, 2019. https://www.prweb.com/releases/global_workplace_analytics_flexjobs_report_159_percent_increase_in_remote_work_since_2005/prweb16471457.htm.

Hering, Beth Braccio. "The History of Telecommuting and Where It Stands Now." Flexjobs. Accessed August 16, 2021. https://www.flexjobs.com/blog/post/the-history-of-telecommuting-stands-now/.

Marinova, Iva. "28 Need-To-Know Remote Work Statistics of 2021." *Review 42 (blog)*. July 4, 2021. https://review42.com/resources/remote-work-statistics/.

Montana Department of Labor and Industry: Remote Workforce Toolkit
https://wsd.dli.mt.gov/employers/remote-workforce-toolkit.

Pelta, Rachel. "FlexJobs Survey: Productivity, Work-Life Balance Improves During Pandemic." Flexjobs. Accessed October 10, 2021.

Powers, Tara. "A Brief History of Virtual Teams." *A Brief History of Virtual Teams (blog)*. June 27, 2018.
https://www.powersresourcecenter.com/brief-history-of-virtual-teams/.

Sword, Alexander. "77% of Workers Say Remote Working Boosts Productivity." *Techmonitor (blog)*. Last modified August 19, 2016. Accessed August 16, 2021.
https://techmonitor.ai/techonology/software/77-of-workers-say-remote-working-boosts-productivity-4514663.

CHAPTER 1 UNLOCKING THE MIND FOR SUCCESS

Campbell, PsyD, Celeste. "What is Neuroplasticity?". *Brainline: All About Brain Injury and PTSD (blog)*. Last Modified July 26, 2018.
https://www.brainline.org/author/celeste-campbell/qa/what-neuroplasticity.

Derler, Andrea, Emily Sanders, and Barbara Steel. "Transforming Performance Management with a Growth Mindset Approach." January 2019.

https://www.researchgate.net/publication/338689101_Transforming_Performance_Management_with_a_Growth_Mindset_Approach.

Ivanenko, Dmitri. "Empty Your Cup - 2012 Movie." September 10, 2017. Video, 0:33.
https://youtu.be/mbk_BX_noXQ.

Dweck, Carol. *The Perils and Promises of Praise.* October 2007.

Dweck, Carol. "The Power of Believing That You Can Improve." Filmed December 2014 at TEDxNorrkoping. Video, 10:11. https://www.ted.com/talks/carol_dweck_the_power_of_believing_that_you_can_improve/transcript?language=en#t-1498.

Dweck, C., M. Murphy, J. Chatman, & L. Kray. (n.d.). "Why Fostering a Growth Mindset in Organizations Matters." Senn Delaney. Retrieved from http://knowledge.senndelaney.com/docs/thought_papers/pdf/stanford_agilitystudy_hart.pdf

(PDF) Growth Mindset Culture. Available from: https://www.researchgate.net/publication/337772472_Growth_Mindset_Culture [accessed Aug 29 2021].

Hochanadel, Aaron and Dora Finamore. "Fixed and Growth Mindset in Education and How Grit Helps Students Persist in the Face of Adversity." Journal of International Education Research, v11, n1, First Quarter 2015: p. 47-50. https://files.eric.ed.gov/fulltext/EJ1051129.pdf.

"How a Growth Mindset and Neuroplasticity Boosts Learning." *Grape Seed English for Children* (blog). September 30, 2020. https://grapeseed.com/us/blog/how-a-growth-mindset-and-neuroplasticity-boosts-learning/.

Kouzes, Tae Kyung, and Barry Z. Posner. "Influence of Managers' Mindset on Leadership Behavior." *Leadership & Organization Development Journal 40(8):829-844.* http://dx.doi.org/10.1108/LODJ-03-2019-0142.

Stanford Alumni. "Developing a Growth Mindset with Carol Dweck." October 9, 2014. Video 9:37. https://youtu.be/hiiEeMN7vbQ.

Talks at Google. "The Growth Mindset." July 16, 2015. Video, 47:25. https://youtu.be/-71zdXCMU6A.

CHAPTER 2 THE LOVING BRAIN

Accenture. *Virtual Ways of Working: Creating a Thriving Digital Culture for Nonprofit Organizations, COVID-19: What to Do Now, What to Do Next.* June, 2020. https://www.accenture.com/_acnmedia/PDF-127/Accenture-Virtual-Ways-Working.pdf.

Bradberry, Dr. Travis. "Are You Emotionally Intelligent? Here's How to Know for Sure." *TalentSmartEQ (blog).* Accessed October 12, 2021. https://www.talentsmarteq.com/articles/Are-You-Emotionally-Intelligent--Here's-How-to-Know-for-Sure-2102500910-p-1.html/.

Cavallo, Kathleen and Dottie Brienza. "Emotional Competence and Leadership Excellence at Johnson & Johnson: The Emotional Intelligence and Leadership Study." *Europe's Journal of Psychology 2(1)*. February 2006. DOI:10.5964/ejop.v2i1.313.

Gautam, Indu and Charu Khurana. "Impact of Emotional Intelligence on the Development of Leadership Skills-A Literature Review." Conference: Vision Uttarakhand 2040: Agenda for Socio-Economic Development at: Dehradun. May 2019. https://www.researchgate.net/publication/333455110_Impact_of_Emotional_Intelligence_on_the_Development_of_Leadership_Skills-A_Literature_Review.

Kannaiah, Dr. Desti and Shanthi, Dr. R.. "A Study on Emotional Intelligence at Work Place." *European Journal of Business and Management* ISSN 2222-1905 (Paper) ISSN 2222-2839 (Online) Vol. 7, No. 24, 2015. https://researchonline.jcu.edu.au/40340/1/40340%20Kannaiah%20and%20Shanthi%20 2015.pdf.

McAllister, Daniel J. "Affect- and Cognition-Based Trust as Foundations for Interpersonal Cooperation in Organizations." The Academy of Management Journal, Vol. 38, No. 1 (Feb., 1995): p. 24-59
https://www.jstor.org/stable/pdf/256727.pdf?casa_token=5pToaVpKocAAAAAA:HVu-XozUVPOOibKtXm-DKPoMsl7QW6G-ny_PKEE6RNME4Q7N-3mfqbuA_2bAoLsvIroKU_A4r45NrHmbIqD_YjELd6HfsBGwvItZSaxdpkBTwIYIsk7s.

Poston, Bob. "Maslow's Hierarchy of Needs." Association of Surgical Technologists. (2009): p. 2. https://www.ast.org/pdf/308.pdf.

Prati, L. Melita, Ceasar Douglas, Gerald R. Ferris, Anthony P. Ammete, and M. Ronald Buckley. "Emotional Intelligence, Leadership Effectiveness, and Team Outcomes.". *International Journal of Organizational Analysis* 11(1): p. 21-40. December 2003. DOI: 10.1108/eb028961.

Srivastava, Kalpana. "Emotional Intelligence and Organizational Effectiveness" *Ind Psychiatry J*. 2013 Jul-Dec; 22(2): p. 97–99. Doi: 10.4103/0972-6748.132912.

Tedx Talks. "Increase Your Self-awareness with One Simple Fix | Tasha Eurich | TEDxMileHigh." Dec 19, 2017. Video 17:17. https://youtu.be/tGdsOXZpyWE.

CHAPTER 3 IMPLEMENTING THE SMART HEART

Gaunt, Derek. Interview by Erik Koester. November 4, 2020. https://www.dropbox.com/s/q4mb2ib6qfsx7si/Derek%20Gaunt%20-%20Creator%20Series%20-%2011-4-2020.mp4?dl=0.

Virtual Not Distant. "WLP248 Emotional Intelligence in Remote Teams." September 17, 2020. Video, 55:33. https://youtu.be/o2tWdMqW9F4.

CHAPTER 4 RECIPROCITY OF TRUST

Baladia, Nuno. "How to Build Trust in the Remote "Workplace": The Future of Work is Trust, Not Tracking." *Ambition & Balance by Moist* (blog). Accessed August 16, 2021. https://blog.doist.com/trust-remote-workplace/.

Blanchard, Kenneth and Spencer Johnson. *The One Minute Manager.* William Morrow & Co, 1982.

Covey, Stephen M.R. *The SPEED of Trust: The One Thing that Changes Everything.* Free Press, 2008.

DeRosa, Darleen M., Donald A. Hantula, Ned Kock, and John D'Arcy. "Trust and Leadership in Virtual Teamwork: A Media Naturalness Perspective." *Human Resource Management,* Vol.43, Nos. 2 & 3, Summer/Fall 2004: p. 219-232. DOI: 10.1002/hrm.20016.

InsuranceNewsNet. "3 Steps to Accelerate the Speed of Trust … in 3 Minutes — Stephen M.R. Covey." June 29, 2018. Video, 6:26. https://youtu.be/-71zdXCMU6A.

Kanawattanachai, Prasert and Youngjin Yoo. "Dynamic Nature of Trust in Virtual Teams." *The Journal of Strategic Information Systems* Volume 11, Issues 3-4 (December 2002): p. 187-213. https://doi.org/10.1016/S0963-8687(02)00019-7.

LEAD. "The Speed of Trust - Stephen M.R Covey @LEAD Presented by HR.com." April 18, 2016. Video, 25:30. https://youtu.be/lvIEfNyZ8Bo.

Prusak, Larry. "The One Thing That Makes Collaboration Work." *Harvard Business Review* (blog). July 5, 2011. https://hbr.org/2011/07/one-thing-that-makes-collaboration.

Rohman, Jessica. *The Business Case for a High-Trust Culture.* Accessed August 16, 2021. https://s3.amazonaws.com/media.greatplacetowork.com/pdfs/Business+Case+for+a+High-Trust+Culture_081816.pdf.

Zak, Paul J. "Article Psychology The Neuroscience of Trust: Management behaviors that Foster Employee Engagement." *Harvard Business Review*, January-February 2017 P.4.

CHAPTER 5 POWER OF TRUST

Benetytė, Donata, and Gražina Jatuliavičienė. "Building and Sustaining Trust in Virtual Teams within Organizational Context." Regional Formation and Development Studies, 2013, no. 2 (10) p. 27. https://core.ac.uk/download/pdf/233177092.pdf.

ConantLeadership. "52 Quotes About Trust and Leadership." Accessed June 12, 2015. https://conantleadership.com/52-quotes-about-trust-and-leadership/.

Hirsch, Arlene. "Building and Leading High-Performing Remote Teams." *SHRM Better Workplaces Better World* (blog). *SHRM Better Workplaces Better World*, July 15, 2019. https://www.shrm.org/resourcesandtools/hr-topics/technology/pages/building-leading-high-performing-remote-teams.aspx.

Marr, Jen. Interview by Erik Koester. October 19, 2020. https://www.dropbox.com/s/57x1mwtwpiy851x/Jen%20 Marr%20-%20Creator%20Series%20-%2010-19-2020.mp4?dl=0.

Kanawattanachai, Prasert and Youngjin Yoo. "Dynamic Nature of Trust in Virtual Teams." *The Journal of Strategic Information Systems* Volume 11, Issues 3–4 (December 2002): Pages 187-213. https://doi.org/10.1016/S0963-8687(02)00019-7.

Rohman, Jessica. *The Business Case for a High-Trust Culture*. Great Place to Work, 2016.

Zak, Paul J. "Article Psychology the Neuroscience of Trust: Management Behaviors that Foster Employee Engagement." *Harvard Business Review*, January-February 2017: p. 5, 7-8.

CHAPTER 6 SETTING MARGINS

Arizona State University. "Today's Leaders Need Clarity the Most, 2020 Executive of the Year Says." October 27, 2020. https://news.wpcarey.asu.edu/20201027-today's-leaders-need-clarity-most-2020-executive-year-says.

Buffer. "The 2021 State of Remote Work." Accessed September 19, 2021. https://buffer.com/2021-state-of-remote-work.

Bundang, Mark. LinkedIn. Mark Bundang PMP, Bec, MBA. Accessed May 2021.

Greene, Brett. New Tech Northwest. "16 Surprising Stats on Remote Work Burnout." July 21, 2020. https://www.newtechnorthwest.com/16-surprising-stats-on-remote-work-%E2%80%8Dburnout/.

Hirsch, Arlene. "Building and Leading High-Performing Remote Teams." *SHRM Better Workplaces Better World* (blog). *SHRM Better Workplaces Better World*, July 15, 2019. https://www.shrm.org/resourcesandtools/hr-topics/technology/pages/building-leading-high-performing-remote-teams.aspx.

LaBrosse, Michelle. "6 Rules for Better Communication in Virtual Teams." *ComputerWorld* (blog). July 22, 2010. https://www.computerworld.com/article/2519498/6-rules-for-better-communication-in-virtual-teams.html.

Owl Labs. "State of Remote Work 2019." Accessed September 19, 2021. https://resources.owllabs.com/state-of-remote-work/2019.

Sullivan, Thomas. "6 Tips for Managing Virtual Teams." *Hult International Business School* (blog). Accessed September 19, 2021. https://www.hult.edu/blog/6-tips-managing-virtual-teams/.

Wrike. "Remote Work Statistics." Accessed September 27, 2021. https://www.wrike.com/remote-work-guide/remote-work-statistics/.

CHAPTER 7 GRAVITY OF FORTITUDE

American Association of Critical-Care Nurses. *The 4 A's to Rise Above Moral Distress: Addressing Moral Distress Requires Making Changes.* Accessed October 11, 2021.
https://www.emergingrnleader.com/wp-content/uploads/2012/06/4As_to_Rise_Above_Moral_Distress.pdf.

Ancient Greek Philosopher. "Aristotle's Courage: A Clear and Short Explanation." July 17, 2015.
https://www.ancientgreekphilosopher.com/2015/07/17/aristotles-courage-a-clear-and-short-explanation/.

Comstock, Beth. Interview by Erik Koester. January 6, 2021.
https://www.dropbox.com/s/aty1ve5q8wtybv4/2021-01-06%20-%20Beth%20Comstock%20-%20Creator%20Session.mp4?dl=0.

Communique. "Daring Leaders Build Trust by Peeling Away the Armor, Choosing Courage Over Comfort." *Communique*(blog). Accessed September 19, 2021.
https://www.guidedinsights.com/daring-leaders-build-trust-by-peeling-away-the-armor-choosing-courage-over-comfort/.

Edmonson, Cole, "Moral Courage and the Nurse Leader" OJIN: The Online Journal of Issues in Nursing Vol. 15, No. 3, Manuscript 5, p. 1. September 2010. DOI: 10.3912/OJIN.Vol15No03Man05.

George, Bill. "Courage: The Defining Characteristic of Great Leaders." *Forbes* (blog). April 24, 2017. https://www.forbes.com/sites/hbsworkingknowledge/2017/04/24/courage-the-defining-characteristic-of-great-leaders/?sh=4b64284411ca.

Greenberg Ph.D., Melanie. "The Six Attributes of Courage." *Psychology Today* (blog). August 23, 2012. https://www.psychologytoday.com/us/blog/the-mindful-self-express/201208/the-six-attributes-courage.

Oxford Lexico. "Courage." Accessed September 21, 2021. https://www.lexico.com/definition/courage.

Putman, Daniel. "Psychological Courage." *Philosophy, Psychiatry, & Psychology,* 4(1) March 1997: p. 1–11. https://doi.org/10.1353/ppp.1997.0008.

Turunen, Anniina. "Building Connection and Courageous Leadership in a Virtual World." *Howspace* (blog). April 27, 2021. https://www.howspace.com/resources/building-leadership-in-a-virtual-world.

Younie, Louise. "Vulnerable Leadership." *London J Prim Care (Abingdon).* May 2, 2016; 8(3): p. 37–38. doi: 10.1080/17571472.2016.1163939.

CHAPTER 8 PROFESSIONAL IDEATION

Fact of the Day 1. "September 30: Lead with Love." September 30, 2020.
https://www.factoftheday1.com/p/lead-with-love.

Goleman, Daniel. "Purpose for the Long Term." *Korn Ferry* (blog). Accessed September 21, 2021.
https://www.kornferry.com/insights/this-week-in-leadership/purpose-for-the-long-term.

Wickman, Gino and Tom Bouwer. *What the Heck is EOS?* BenBella Books, Inc., 2017.

Wrike. "Remote Work Statistics." Accessed September 27, 2021.
https://www.wrike.com/remote-work-guide/remote-work-statistics/.

CHAPTER 9 TO SPEAK OR NOT TO SPEAK

Caggiati, Bree. "How Video Conferencing Powers the Remote Workplace, an Interview with Michael from Zoom." *ShieldGeo: Now Part of Velocity Global* (blog). Accessed September 26, 2021.
https://shieldgeo.com/how-zoom-video-communication-can-help-your-remote-team/.

Caggiati, Bree. "Tips for Communicating with Your Overseas Employees: Insights from an International Business Expert." *ShieldGeo: Now Part of Velocity Global* (blog). April 22, 2019.
https://shieldgeo.com/tips-for-communicating-with-your-overseas-employees-insights-from-an-international-business-expert/.

Denmark, Deloitte. "Leading Virtual Teams: Eight Principles for Mastering Virtual Leadership Teams." *Deloitte* (blog). Accessed September 26, 2021. https://www2.deloitte.com/global/en/pages/about-deloitte/articles/covid-19/leading-virtual-teams.html.

Dhawan, Erica and Tomas Chamorro-Premuzic. "How to Collaborate Effectively If Your Team Is Remote." *Harvard Business Review* (blog). February 27, 2018. https://hbr.org/2018/02/how-to-collaborate-effectively-if-your-team-is-remote.

FOND. "Managing a Virtual Team: 5 Ways to Build Culture." Accessed September 22, 2021. https://www.fond.co/resources/managing-a-virtual-team/.

Grow. "7 Communication Secrets of Effective Remote Teams." *Grow* (blog). August 23, 2019. https://grow360.com/blog/7-communication-secrets-of-effective-remote-teams.

Hastwell, Claire. "6 Tips for Better Communication with Remote Teams." *Great Place to Work* (blog). Accessed September 26, 2021. https://www.greatplacetowork.com/resources/blog/7-tips-for-better-communication-with-remote-teams.

LaBrosse, Michelle. "6 Rules for Better Communication in Virtual Teams." *ComputerWorld* (blog). July 22, 2010. https://www.computerworld.com/article/2519498/6-rules-for-better-communication-in-virtual-teams.html.

Meier, J.D. "The Best Lessons I Learned from Bill Gates." *Sources of Insight: Insight and Action for Work and Life* (blog). Accessed September 26, 2021. https://sourcesofinsight.com/lessons-learned-from-bill-gates/.

Newman, Sean A., Robert C. Ford, and Greg W. Marshall. "Virtual Team Leader Communication: Employee Perception and Organizational Reality." *Sage Journals*. February 2019: p. 4. https://doi.org/10.1177/2329488419829895.

Riordan, Monica. "Emojis as Tools for Emotion Work: Communicating Affect in Text Messages." *Sage Journals* April 2017: p. 12. *https://doi.org/10.1177/0261927X17704238.*

Riordan, Monica. "The Communicative Role of Non-Face Emojis: Affect and Disambiguation." *Science Direct,* Computers in Human Behavior. Vol. 76 (November 2017): p. 75-86. https://doi.org/10.1016/j.chb.2017.07.009.

TEDx Talks. "The Power of Listening | William Ury | TEDxSanDiego." January 7, 2015. Video, 15:40. https://youtu.be/saXfavo1OQo.

The Challenges of Working in Virtual Teams: Virtual Team Survey Report - 2010. 55 Fifth Ave., New York, NY: RW3 Culture Wizard, 2010.

CHAPTER 10 ENVIRONMENT CULTIVATION

Buffer. "State of Remote Work: How Remote Workers from around the World Feel about Remote Work, the Benefits and Struggles That Come along with It, and What It's Like to Be a Remote Worker in 2019." Accessed September 21, 2021. https://buffer.com/state-of-remote-work-2019.

Chierotti, Logan. "Virtual Teams: 10 Tips to Creating a Strong Work Culture with Online Business and Remote Teams Becoming the Norm, Developing a Stellar Virtual Culture Is More Important than Ever." *Inc.* (blog). March 17, 2017. https://www.inc.com/logan-chierotti/10-ways-to-create-a-strong-work-culture-for-virtual-teams.html.

Dugan, Katherine and Varun Bhatnagar. "Virtually Alone: Real Ways to Connect Remote Teams." *Strategy+Business* (blog). June 25, 2018. https://www.strategy-business.com/article/Virtually-Alone-Real-Ways-to-Connect-Remote-Teams.

FOND. "Managing a Virtual Team: 5 Ways to Build Culture." Accessed September 22, 2021. https://www.fond.co/resources/managing-a-virtual-team/.

Forbes Technology Council. "13 Ways Tech Leaders Can Build a Strong Culture in a Remote Team." *Forbes* (blog). January 5, 2021. https://www.forbes.com/sites/forbestechcouncil/2021/01/05/13-ways-tech-leaders-can-build-a-strong-culture-in-a-remote-team/?sh=51b79406bc66.

Gardner, Heidi K. and Ivan Matviak. "Coronavirus Could Force Teams to Work Remotely." *Harvard Business Review* (blog). March 5, 2020. https://hbr.org/2020/03/coronavirus-could-force-teams-to-work-remotely.

Kane, Nick. "How to Coach Your Team Remotely." *Training Industry* (blog). April 8, 2020. https://trainingindustry.com/articles/sales/how-to-coach-your-team-remotely/.

Kurter, Heidi Lynne. "5 Ways to Nurture a Virtual Culture That Keeps Employees Connected." *Forbes* (blog). April 10, 2020. https://www.forbes.com/sites/heidilynnekurter/2020/04/10/5-ways-to-nurture-a-virtual-culture-that-keeps-employees-connected/?sh=41a12566587d.

Roberts, Wess. *Leadership Secrets of Attila the Hun*. Warner Books, Inc., 1987.

Startupfood. "How to Build a Strong Culture with Remote Employees - By Elizabeth Hall, VP of People at Trello." June 30, 2016. Video, 29:40. https://youtu.be/6wy5dahX2ZM.

Huffman, Steve. Interview by Erik Koester. May 8, 2021. . https://www.dropbox.com/s/6ei06gqok11bide/2021-03-08%20-%20Steve%20Huffman%20-%20Creator%20Session.mp4?dl=0.

Trueman, Charlotte. "Remote Working: Is It Doing More Harm than Good?" *Forbes* (blog).
https://www.techadvisor.com/feature/small-business/remote-working-is-it-doing-more-harm-than-good-3789115/.

Wingard, Jason. "Leading Remote Workers: The Coronavirus' Impact on Effective Management." *Forbes* (blog). March 13, 2020.
https://www.forbes.com/sites/jasonwingard/2020/03/13/team-working-at-home-because-of-coronavirus-heres-how-to-lead-them-effectively/?sh=c482f8f31628.

CHAPTER 11 THE GUARDIAN

Derler, Andrea, Emily Sanders, and Barbara Steel. "Transforming Performance Management with a Growth Mindset Approach." January 2019.
https://www.researchgate.net/publication/338689101_Transforming_Performance_Management_with_a_Growth_Mindset_Approach.

Cherry, Kendra. "8 Characteristics of Authoritarian Parenting." *Verywellmind* (blog). June 28, 2020.
https://www.verywellmind.com/what-is-authoritarian-parenting-2794955.

Cherry, Kendra. "Authoritative Parenting Characteristics and Effects." *Verywellmind* (blog). September 17, 2020.
https://www.verywellmind.com/what-is-authoritative-parenting-2794956.

Cherry, Kendra. *Parenting Styles: The Four Styles of Parenting.* About.com, 2014. http://www.kvccdocs.com/KVCC/2017-Summer/PSY215/lessons/L-16/Results-of-Parenting.pdf

Cherry, Kendra. "Permissive Parenting Characteristics and Effects." *Verywellmind* (blog). April 29, 2021. https://www.verywellmind.com/what-is-permissive-parenting-2794957.

Cherry, Kendra. "Why Parenting Styles Matter When Raising Children." *Verywellmind* (blog). April 14, 2020. https://www.verywellmind.com/parenting-styles-2795072.

Govindaraju, Madhukar. "Peer Coaching- a Must-Have for Your Remotely Distributed Team." *Numly* (blog). February 17, 2021. https://www.numly.io/blog/peer-coaching-a-must-have-for-your-remotely-distributed-team/.

Hurst, Aaron. "Newly Remote Workers Need Peer Coaching." *MITSloan Management Review* (blog). April 20, 2020. https://sloanreview.mit.edu/article/newly-remote-workers-need-peer-coaching/.

Lew, Claire. "Remote Leadership Training: How to Best Support Your Remote Managers." *Know Your Team* (blog). December 10, 2020. https://knowyourteam.com/blog/2020/12/10/remote-leadership-training-how-to-best-support-your-remote-managers/.

Musashi, Miyamoto. *The Real Art of Japanese Management.* Bantam Books, 1982.

Startupfood. "How to Build Your Culture When Employees Work Remotely - by Rodolphe Dutel, bizzdev @Buffer." December 9, 2015. Video, 45:47.
https://youtu.be/7JwcS6Iktto. (youtube)

Stobierski, Tim. "5 Pros & Cons of Authoritative Leadership." *Harvard Business School Online* (blog). November 12, 2019.
https://online.hbs.edu/blog/post/authoritative-leadership-style.

Thompson, Gregg. "How to Coach Employees from a Distance." *Remote Leadership Institute* (blog). Accessed September 21, 2021.
https://www.remoteleadershipinstitute.com/communication/coach-employees-distance/.

Whitener, Svetlana. "To Be a More Effective Leader, Take a Page from Your Parenting Style." *Forbes* (blog). May 7, 2019.
https://www.forbes.com/sites/forbescoachescouncil/2019/05/07/to-be-a-more-effective-leader-take-a-page-from-your-parenting-style/?sh=7ecdc5eb7196.

CHAPTER 12 FUTURE OF REMOTE WORK

Goleman, Daniel. "Don't Think Purpose is Important? Gen Zers Do." *Korn Ferry* (blog). Accessed September 21, 2021.
https://www.kornferry.com/insights/this-week-in-leadership/dont-think-purpose-is-important-gen-zers-do.

Goleman, Daniel. "Purpose for the Long Term." *Korn Ferry* (blog). Accessed September 21, 2021.
https://www.kornferry.com/insights/this-week-in-leadership/purpose-for-the-long-term.

Kelly, Jack. "Survey Asks Employees at Top U.S. Companies if They'd Give Up $30,000 to Work from Home: The Answers May Surprise You." *Forbes* (blog). May 21, 2021. https://www.forbes.com/sites/jackkelly/2021/05/21/survey-asks-employees-at-top-us-companies-if-theyd-give-up-30000-to-work-from-home-the-answers-may-surprise-you/?sh=78614dad330f.

MBO Partners. "Digital Nomads: Leading the Shift to Remote and Distributed Work." Accessed September 21, 2021. https://www.mbopartners.com/state-of-independence/2019-digital-nomad-research/.

McKinsey & Company. "What's Next for Remote Work: An Analysis of 2,000 Tasks, 800 Jobs, and Nine Countries." November 23, 2020. https://www.mckinsey.com/featured-insights/future-of-work/whats-next-for-remote-work-an-analysis-of-2000-tasks-800-jobs-and-nine-countries.

Roberts, Shannon. LinkedIn. Accessed February 2021.

State of Remote Work: How Remote Workers from around the World Feel about Remote Work, the Benefits and Struggles That Come along with It, and What It's Like to Be a Remote Worker in 2019. Buffer:2019. https://buffer.com/state-of-remote-work-2019.

Wu, Jun. "A Deep Dive into Remote Work for Our Future of Work." *Forbes* (blog). March 9, 2020. https://www.forbes.com/sites/cognitiveworld/2020/03/09/a-deep-dive-into-remote-work-for-our-future-of-work/?sh=52ce43471843.

www.ingramcontent.com/pod-product-compliance
Lightning Source LLC
LaVergne TN
LVHW011816060526
838200LV00053B/3798